In Spite of the System

In Spite of the System

The Individual and Educational Reform

Bernard C. Watson

Ballinger Publishing Company • Cambridge, Mass.
A Subsidiary of J.B. Lippincott Company

International Standard Book Number: 0-88410-159-2

Library of Congress Catalog Card Number: 74-16370

Printed in the United States of America

Library of Congress Cataloging in Publication Data

Watson, Bernard C
    In spite of the system.

    Includes bibliographical references.
    1. Minorities–Education–United States. 2. Public schools–United States.
I. Title.
LC3731.W37   370.19'34   74-16370
ISBN 0-88410-159-2

Dedicated to Barbra and Chuckie

.... Even in the darkest of times we have the right to expect some illumination ... such illumination may well come less from theories and concepts than from the uncertain, flickering, and often weak light that some men and women, in their lives and their works, will kindle under almost all circumstances and shed over the time span that was given them on earth. .... Eyes so used to darkness as ours will hardly be able to tell whether their light was the light of a candle or that of a blazing sun. But such objective evaluation seems to me a matter of secondary importance which can be safely left to posterity.

Hannah Arendt, *Men in Dark Times*

Table of Contents

60538

Preface

Over the past ten years the American public has been exposed to a series of books and articles which purport to chronicle the lifeless, boring stultifying, and dehumanizing nature of public schools in urban and rural areas. Poor children, black children, Chicano and Puerto Rican children, native American children and others are pictured as helpless pawns in a rigidly structured bureaucratic system. Teachers and school administrators are often portrayed as automatons, devoid of ideals, feeling, and the most basic elements of human compassion. In such a system, staffed by such people it is argued, youthful ambition, native intelligence, nascent creativity and curiosity, and basic hope in the future are destroyed. Only by revolutionizing the educational system and imposing change from the outside can these conditions be altered argue some of the critics. Others suggest that a new breed of young, commited teachers and administrators, freed from the rigidities of credentialism and oppressive administration, will lead us to the promised land of relevant, effective public education. Clearly, most seem to agree, the present system and its staff can play no significant part in bringing about the needed changes and improvements.

But who are these authors, these critics who have written many of the popular and best selling treatises? Most of them are well educated and fairly young, having taken their degrees from some of the best colleges and universities in the country. Most of them are comfortable with the English language; they write well, and they are articulate and passionate in their commitment, particularly in speeches, seminars, and talk shows. I believe most of them are sincere in their concerns. But many have only a perfunctory knowledge of the real world of public schools. If they have experience as teachers, that experience is limited to a few years in the classroom, usually no more than two or three years. Following this experience, they rarely return to teaching unless it is at the college or university level. In some instances, they do return to teaching at the elementary or secondary level, but it is more often than not in "free" schools or alternative schools or "open" private schools which serve limited numbers of the children they were so concerned about in their articles and books.

But they continue to write and in so doing reveal an important slice of reality to us all. Their books and articles tell the stories of young idealistic teachers journeying to the backwoods of a southern state and teaching ignorant, economically deprived black children; of a young, well-educated teacher who labored in the classrooms of black and Spanish Harlem; of a young idealistic Harvard graduate who taught for a year in an elementary school in Boston; of how a young idealistic woman teacher coped with a large urban school in the ghetto. And through it all one gets the feeling that some minor gains can be made, but the problems are really too massive and one should have little hope that major improvements can or will be made. The individual teacher or administrator, however committed or skillful, will, at best, delay or soften the ultimate result. It is a dismal picture, discouraging and debilitating.

Yet, this is only a part of the picture. Researchers gather and analyze data on large numbers of children, on entire school systems, on aggregate numbers of teacher and administrator characteristics, on school climate, teacher turnover, administrative style, achievement scores, intelligence quotients, college attendance, and a host of other variables. For urban and rural schools, their conclusions are not very encouraging. For the poor and black and Spanish-speaking minorities, they are positively frightening. Perhaps the isolated pictures drawn by the individual authors is supported by massive data from the macro system.

But there is another slice of reality which is rarely mentioned, let alone written about and published. It is a slice of reality rarely if ever examined by researchers; funding for this kind of research is not usually available. The reality referred to here is the real world of the public school teacher and administrator. These teachers and administrators are not writers; they are doers, activists. They do not have the time or the inclination to write about their experiences, their battles, accomplishments and failures. They give few speeches, except to the PTA or to assemblies of students. They have labored and continue to labor in the grimy trenches of public education in poor areas, in cities, in rural villages. They are people who, for the most part, do not have the option to enter other careers; perhaps most would not choose to do so if they could They have made major contributions, but they remain anonymous. Yet there is much we can learn from them. Their contributions were made in the one-room schoolhouses in the rural south when there was dual system of education. They were made in the "blackboard jungles" of the big cities, in the under-financed, undercapitalized black, private, and public colleges, in the oases of compassion and learning in Appalachia, in the single classroom of Public School,

U.S.A. All of these individuals shared one thing in common: they believed that one individual could make a difference. They understood—some intellectually, some emotionally—that the system is not a disemboweled entity with a life of its own; it is all of us. Because they believed this and acted upon it, it seems to me important that their individual efforts and successes be highlighted.

Today, as it has been throughout our history, most poor and minority parents have no choice but to send their children to the public schools. Alternatives in the private sector are not feasible for most. The history of free schools is not particularly encouraging. They tend to be underfinanced, serve limited numbers of children, have a short life span of approximately three to four years, and tend not to deal, in a systematic way, with the realities of credentialism. They have little access to other more formal institutions, and make few linkages with the public schools, which are likely to continue to exist as the primary institution providing elementary and secondary education for most children, particularly the poor. State legislatures, city councils, and state departments of education have, thus far, given little indication that they are inclined to seriously consider alternative ways of providing basic education to most of its citizens. Universities, colleges, and teacher training institutions seem ill disposed to view private and/or parochial schools as viable alternatives to public schools in the cities or the suburbs. It seems, therefore, that whether significant improvements in public education occur or are possible will depend in large measure on what teachers, counselors, administrators, paraprofessionals, and others find it possible to do within the context of the system, however it is organized.

Included in this book are the stories of several people who have made and are making a difference. What is described is the way it really happened. The names and places have been changed in order that the importance of their deeds be highlighted. Obviously, others could have been included in this narrative. A chart describing a few of the other programs that might have been included appears in the Appendix. The people discussed in some detail happen to be three with whom the author was most familiar. Moreover, the decision was made to discuss these three because they were people who, by virtue of their roles as leaders of schools or programs and because of their unusual commitments and personalities, were able to exert greater influence over numbers of children than could an individual classroom teacher.

Even if it were possible to conduct a detailed and sophisticated anslysis of the three institutions and the key individuals, the results would probably not lead to a grand design or a formula to revolutionize public education or solve its persistent problems. But then neither has anything else, to my knowledge. We could obviously learn more and prescribe better if all of the data were available. How much more and how much better, I am not sure. It may be that the individual is most important; his or her goals, commitment, skill, and persistence. In any case, I am telling these stories because I have to;

they are an important piece of reality. My sincere wish is that they may give hope to a student, a parent, or a teacher.

I wish to express my appreciation to the following persons: Lynn Bendann, Dorothy Blanchard, Robert Ferrara, Faustine Jones, Lonni Moseley and William Stinson. Without their assistance, the book would not have been completed.

In Spite of the System

Chapter One

Does Education Make a Difference

INTRODUCTION

For the past decade a debate has been raging in this country. Ignored by and unknown to most Americans, it finally penetrated the consciousness of the man in the street when daily newspapers began to report and serialize a book written by Christopher Jencks, *Inequality*. Simply stated, the major thesis of the book was that education made little difference in reducing inequality, educational or otherwise. And further, adding more money to public school budgets would do little to equalize opportunity and life chances between the affluent and poor, black and white. And thus the issue was joined in public debate.

But Jencks' book was only the latest of a series of social science documents and theories. Daniel Moynihan's *Maximum Feasible Misunderstanding,*[1] Edward Banfield's *The Unheavenly City,*[2] and Nathan Glazer's "The Limits of Social Policy,"[3] to name a few, had all contributed individually and collectively to the effort by some to roll back governmental attempts to improve the lot of minorities and the poor. Simultaneously, from another vantage point, there was a resurgence of the old/new theories of racial superiority/inferiority stated most openly by Authur Jensen,[4] William Shockley,[5] Richard Herrenstein,[6] and H.J. Eysenck.[7] And gilding the lily were the counsels of Herbert Kohl,[8] who advised that one good year was not enough, and Jonathan Kozol,[9] who informed us that schools were racist, brutal, joyless killers of intelligence, youthful creativity, and institutions of stultifying conformity. And as if these were not sufficient to destroy all hope for the average citizen, advice from the wings told us that deschooling was the answer; decentralization and community control, alternative education, free schools and eliminating the mindlessness of educators would lead us to the promised land. Lower the age for compulsory attendance some advised, create a new breed of teacher and administrator, reduce the size of classes and/or schools. Go to the market place: create a voucher system so parents can purchase the education they desire for their children. Desegregate. Integrate. Separate the boys from girls. Create open classrooms. But remember, counsel the modern day sophists, education doesn't really make that much difference.

This whole dialogue is mind boggling to many Americans who have always believed that education made a difference. It was more than a belief, it was an article of faith. At almost any other time in our history, serious discussion of whether education makes a difference would have been unthinkable. It would have been met with suspicion, incredulity or mystification. Does education make a difference? One might as well ask whether food, sleep or oxygen make a difference.

Of course, we are not really talking about education, which is not limited to what takes place in schools, but about schooling. That is what is under discussion (one might almost say under attack) today: The whole complex process whereby children and young people are sent to certain buildings and required to spend eight or twelve or sixteen years acquiring certain skills and understandings under the direction of certain people labeled teachers, administrators, and supervisors.

One may argue, with considerable justification, about whether some schools are better than others, or one might even discuss the proposition that formal schooling as we know it is antithetical to good education. The response to this seems obvious. Certainly some schools are better than others. Why else would families who have the option to decide where and how their children are to be educated automatically gravitate to neighborhoods where schools have a reputation for high teaching standards, good administration, or fine facilities? Or why would well-to-do families send their youngsters, who have the benefit of every imaginable "cultural advantage" at home, to private schools nearby or to the great boarding schools such as Groton, St. Paul's, and Miss Porter's? There seems to be no question in the minds of these families about whether education makes a difference: they willingly pay exorbitant sums—in high suburban tax rates or in tuition bills or both—to obtain the best kind of education available. And they certainly do not rely on their children's ability to simply absorb, by a kind of osmosis, the intellectual and cultural skills which they will later need to run family corporations or become successful professional men.

If we look back through history, we find no evidence to indicate that anyone has ever seriously raised the question with which American citizens are asked to deal today. Quite the contrary. Political philosophers, beginning with Plato and Aristotle, have usually devoted much of their teaching to education, on the assumption that the state's health and welfare depend on the proper training of the young in the duties of citizenship. Indeed, education has been seen as the key to enabling men to become fully human, to exercise their peculiarly human attribute of rationality. Similarly, religious teachers have always urged on parents their duty to train their children in the traditions and precepts of their religion. Without education, it seemed obvious that neither the church nor the state could long survive.

Think of how education has been viewed by the aspiring poor of every age and nation. Think of the stories we have all heard—some may be part of ones own family history—of parents who struggled and saved and even scrimped on necessities in order to see that their youngsters made it to school, or to college, or to the university. It never occurred to them that education made "no difference"—they *knew* that it was the key to security and status that they had never known but which their educated children could enjoy. Education has, of course, been feared by members of some ruling elites: they knew all too well that education was a liberating force which, if put in the hands of slaves and peasants, might well turn the world upside down. Rightly perceiving that education was threatening to their own designs, they burned books, closed schools and universities, and generally reserved educational opportunity to the chosen few who could be counted on to be loyal to the goals of the existing regime. Other rulers have turned education to their own ends by insisting that the young be indoctrinated with political propaganda, along with reading and arithmetic. (To an extent, all societies do this. After all, schooling is one of the primary means of socialization in every society.)

It is incredible that something that "makes no difference" should have been viewed for so long as both threat and promise; should have absorbed so much of the time and energy of so many. Whatever we are, whatever we have accomplished, is a tribute to the power of education, broadly conceived. One generation after another has absorbed the learning of the past, moved beyond it or added to it, and passed on to their children not only their own knowledge, but the thirst for more. Why, then, is the question being asked: Does education make a difference? Partly, no doubt, it is a symptom of the temper of our time—when most traditions, conventions, and commonly accepted values are subject to doubt and questioning, or are even being abandoned. But even more significant, the question is evidence of the social and political reaction which is rampant in this country at present. It is raised—scornfully by some, hesitantly or sadly by others—as a challenge to the most basic of American beliefs: the belief that through education a society of free men might have equal opportunity to succeed in life and, even more important, to maintain control over their chosen government.

But before we explore the reasons *why* this question is being posed at this particular time and in this context, it seems appropriate to attempt to respond to it directly. Does education make a difference? Or, in other words, what evidence is available on the success of education in achieving its objectives? One way to approach this is to take the question apart and look at each of its key components in turn. First, what kind of "evidence" is being requested? What will satisfy the judge and jurors? It has previously been indicated that history is replete with examples of how education did, in fact, make all the difference. Let us remember the persistence with which the former slaves (and their abolitionist allies) struggled to get schools and teachers—although they were confronted at every turn by scorn, contempt, patronizing words, and outright refusals to have tax monies used for the education of former slaves. As early as 1866, the various freedmen's associations had established nearly 1,000 schools attended by some 90,000 pupils—a number which increased to almost 112,000 the following year. James McPherson, the Princeton historian, noting that "the children came from a cultural environment almost entirely devoid of intellectual stimulation," says that progress was slow—but he adds:

> The freedmen had an almost passionate desire to learn to read and write, and children laboriously taught their parents the alphabet and multiplication tables during their spare time. Teachers invariably testified that despite their disadvantages in background, training and environment, Negro children learned to read almost as well and as rapidly as white children.[10]

Despite the collapse of Reconstruction and the ensuing establishment of strict segregation and dual facilities, the proportion of the black population attending school climbed steadily. Black people knew that education made a difference—and so did their oppressors. Gunnar Myrdal, in his classic book *An American Dilemma,* describes the abysmal conditions in black schools in the South during the 1930s. He writes:

> ... Negro education still does not have a fixed legitimate acknowledged place. It is realized that something must be done in order to keep the Negro satisfied and in order to uphold the American slogan of free schools for every child, but it is rare that a community has any real interest in planning or building a wise system of education for the race. Politically, it is not admitted that a Negro has a right to schools. . . .[11]

Those who carefully engineered an inferior school system for blacks—(a program whose nature and extent has been well documented not only by Myrdal, but by such other scholars as Ambrose Caliver, Horace Mann Bond, and Henry Allen Bullock)—whether in the rural South or urban North knew very well the power and liberating force inherent in education. Had schooling been made available to the black child on the same terms as to the white, the myth of his inferiority would very quickly have been shattered.[12]

Yet many of the youngsters did manage to complete this inadequate schooling and went on to the black colleges, which for the last century have provided almost the sole opportunity for higher or professional education available to blacks. Indeed, as late as 1969, Meharry and Howard were educating all but a tiny number of black medical and dental students, and 27 percent of all black law students were enrolled in four black schools.[13] Without these institutions, the black community would have been almost completely without medical and legal services—which are still much scarcer for minorities than for the white population of this country. One must ask again: how is it possible to entertain the possibility that education makes no difference? The oppressed and ignorant slaves knew better, and generations of their descendants, whether themselves graduates of universities or simply beneficiaries of the specialized training of fellow blacks, know better.

Similarly, the thousands upon thousands of immigrants who came to these shores, fleeing from famine and oppression elsewhere, counted on education to break down language barriers, to help them adapt to the customs and culture of their newly adopted land. And, whether in formal or informal settings, these people and even more their children, quickly (though not always without pain and stress) adopted American ways. What evidence do we have that education succeeds? They would point to their sons and grandsons who, within a generation, began to take their places as respected citizens, landowners, and professional men in the new country.

If one prefers another kind of evidence, why not recall the critical role education has played in meeting various national goals? In wartime, for instance, workers were trained without previous factory experience (many of them housewives and adolescents) to operate complex machinery; youthful officers were taught to become fluent in another language, in only months; jets and rockets and the atom bomb were developed; crass youth were taught to build, operate, and maintain the most complicated equipment in the history of man. Our feelings about war may be more ambiguous now than in the 1940s when we were in a desperate race with time and the most efficient and educated war machine ever established. Without the determination and ability to educate our people to meet the crisis, history might have run a very different course.

More specific evidence can be found, however, in the history of agriculture: Five percent of the population of this country feeds the other 95 percent. The unusually high standard of living enjoyed in this country could not have been achieved had we not discovered how to provide for this most basic of human needs—food. It was not done by accident, but through education: think of the role played by the land-grant colleges, the agricultural extension stations and labs, the field agents, who trained farmers in new methods and machinery by which they could increase their land's yield. In other parts of the world today, one hears of the "green revolution"—discoveries from scientists which are helping to ameliorate the ancient spectre of famine. Agricultural education has already accomplished much in some of the Third World countries—and now that indigenous farmers have learned to operate modern equipment, they require further education in order to be able to maintain it.

One hardly needs to mention the space program—so clear is the relationship to education. A single space shot, the Russian Sputnik, was responsible for widespread curriculum changes in this country. And in turn, the graduates of our science programs—engineering, biology, chemistry, and a host of other specialities whose names one has difficulty pronouncing, let alone understanding—succeeded within ten short years in breaking the barrier between man and the moon. What evidence do we have about the difference made by education? What more evidence do we need?

If statistical evidence is more convincing, that, too, can be provided. Henry Levin, Stanford economist, and his colleagues put together a study not long ago for the Mondale Committee—and calculated that inadequate education (which they defined as less than high school completion) for working-age males in this country would cost, over their lifetimes, some $237 billion in lost income, $71 billion in lost tax monies, and some $6 billion in costs for welfare and prison.[14] And very recently, the Census Bureau published a survey establishing the relationships between level of education completed and earning power. The mean annual incomes for each group ranged from $5,950 for those with less than eight years of schooling to $16,698 for those with four or more years of college.[15] These aren't theories, or models, or somebody's projections: these are facts, culled out from the ever growing masses of data collected by the government to let us know what is actually happening to people.

Let us move on to the second key word in the question: "success." How is "success" to be defined? One really can't talk about success in the abstract, because it has to be connected with something else—namely, the objectives one deems appropriate for education. In an admirable move toward defining educational objectives more precisely, teachers are sometimes required to specify their goals in behavioral terms, so that one can measure the extent to which they have succeeded or not. But educators often lose sight of the broader role played by the educational system in our society. We take it for granted (although again one must remind himself that perhaps it is no longer taken for granted) that education is the chief, if not the only, means whereby people, especially the poor and minorities prepare for some jobs, increase their income, move upward socially, participate in democratic affairs. Yet there are also the "latent functions" of the vast educational system: to provide a place and activities for those too young to enter on a career; to keep them out of mischief and off the streets; to look after them while parents (and increasingly *both* parents) are at work outside the home, either from necessity or from choice. Some of the more romantic educational philosophers, of course, see and condemn these "latent functions" of education—but they seem ill prepared, despite the flow of rhetoric about schools as prisons, to present workable alternatives for the care and supervision of millions of children.

And let us not forget the schools as employers. They provide jobs and income and status for millions of people and, for the poor and minorities, in particular, a major opportunity for upward mobility. If one were to consider education's success only in performing these latent functions, then our task would be relatively simple. At present, the vast majority of youngsters under sixteen *are* in school, off the streets, and out of the factories. And the few exceptions—children of migrant workers or urban dropouts—are cause for particular concern just because they are exceptions. The school systems, as caretakers of the young and as key employers, are certainly making a difference.

But what about the specifically educational functions? We have all been in conversations where someone launched into a tirade about what the schools should be doing, or what would happen if they would just start doing something else. What do people have in mind when they think of educational "success," even in a vague and general way? Sometimes they seem to mean that one would have total employment: everyone would be working, no one would be on welfare—if the schools were successful. Others seem to have visions, similar to those of the old utilitarians, of universal happiness: no riots, no unrest, no apathy, no alienation—everybody happy. Is that what is meant by success when education is being evaluated? Or is one interested in the relationship between schooling and citizenship, and does one judge successful education, therefore, on the basis of statistics about participation in the last election? Of course, one might feel that education should produce cultured people. One would then measure success by sales of books, or attendance at cultural events, or amount of amateur activity in the arts, crafts, music, and dance.

Obviously, it is not possible to make sense of "success" without specifying education's objectives. But first one must consider the third key word in the question, namely "education." Well, here again one has to ask, what is meant by "education"? Obviously there is a distinction between formal and informal education, and few would deny the critical importance of what is learned informally; in families, over the air waves, on the streets, in movie houses. Some people, in fact, regard this type of learning as so important, so "meaningful" or "relevant" that they would have us abandon the schools so that everyone might devote himself to such informal learning. But we are here concerned with formal education: that which takes place, for the most part, in special buildings under the guidance of specially trained personnel. Still, one needs to ask again specifically, what is meant when one uses the word "education." Are we referring to public or private or parochial education? To elementary, secondary or higher education? To liberal arts or vocational education? And when these questions have been answered, one must still know what kinds of schools one is talking about: rich or poor, in what part of the country, rural or urban? And what kind of atmosphere is in them: mindless or purposeful; permissive or rigidly structured; loving or tension-ridden?

Sloppy writing or speech, old-fashioned English teachers would say, is a sign of sloppy thinking, and I heartily concur, when I hear people ask questions about "education" as though that conveyed to me in and of itself a crystal clear concept which I could then discuss. "Define your terms" has been the first rule for debate since men began to argue, but we still avoid doing so all too often, not least of the reasons being that it is so much easier to talk in generalities, to talk about "Society" or "The Economy" or, as here, "Education."

As noted earlier, "success" in education, as in any other enterprise, is inextricably tied up with "objectives." It is not possible to discuss educational success without reference to educational objectives, goals, and purposes. And although others have developed this point more fully in scholarly discourses, let me mention just two of the most important objectives of the educational process: socializing the individual, and making him, at the same time, self-sufficient.

Societies have used their formal educational system to socialize the young, that is, to indoctrinate them with the values and standards of the group, to teach them to distinguish between acceptable and unacceptable behavior, to give them a sense of pride in the history and traditions of their country. In other words, the young have to learn, and do, to a greater or lesser degree, that they are and will always be dependent on one another. But simultaneously they must also learn to be independent: to develop an identity, a feeling of self-worth, and skills and abilities which will allow them to reach their personal goals. So the broadest objectives of education—socialization and individual self-sufficiency—are frequently in contradiction. But the tension between them can be a creative tension. As the student learns about his group, his society and his country, he also learns to reflect on them, and as he reflects, he criticizes. It is significant that reform, rebellion, and revolution have so often been sponsored and led by students.

Does education make a difference? Most people I know would be surprised to know that this question is being asked, let alone seriously considered. Certainly the minority group members of this society would be astonished. So would the poor, in Appalachia or in the heart of any one of our cities. So would the immigrants to these shores. And farmers and space scientists and oceanographers.

Restating the question doesn't help very much, either. We have looked at another version—What evidence is available of the success of education in meeting its objectives?—and we have seen that each of the key terms is so imprecise that the question as a whole is almost meaningless.

PUBLIC POLICY AND EDUCATION

To what extent is the individual responsible for his own destiny? To what extent is the government responsible for regulating or establishing economic and social institutions to ensure that all individuals have the opportunity to succeed in attaining their goals? When individuals or groups are not successful (relative to others in the society), should the blame be attached to them or those institutions?

The relationship of the individual to the state is the most profound and most difficult of all the problems posed by political philosophy, and it is certainly incapable of solution—or even delineation—in these few brief pages. It is possible, however, to indicate some of the paradoxes in popular attitudes toward the role of government.

Perhaps the most startling contradiction is to be found in nineteenth century American history: devout adherence to the theories of laissez-faire economics, while private fortunes were being established with federal assistance and support. Using as their text the "laws" of the marketplace unveiled by Smith, Ricardo, and Malthus, national leaders proclaimed that inequality of wealth was inevitable, and that to tamper with "the system" would ruin it for everyone, including the workingman. Indeed, the formation of large fortunes by a few was regarded as essential to the continued growth and expansion of capitalism, for only with great resources could men afford to take the risks necessary in new investment and invention. In the years following the Civil War, even the Supreme Court seemed captivated by the enthusiasm of uninhibited commercial expansion and the conquering of the West: as Professor Corwin noted, "it tended to view Congress' power under the 'commerce' clause . . . as primarily a power to foster, protect, and promote commerce,"[16] rather than to regulate.

During this period, however, the financiers, entrepreneurs, and industrial magnates who subscribed wholeheartedly to the tenets of Adam Smith, and who regularly called for individual effort as the divinely appointed way to achieve material success, were more than capable of using governmental power to advance their own "individual" efforts. The Pacific Railway Act of 1862, for example, ceded to the four partners who had formed the Central Pacific Railway Company (Huntington, Hopkins, Stanford, and Crocker) some 4,500,000 acres of public land in the West—this in addition to a subsidy of $24 million of federal funds. Another parcel of land of the same size was subsequently deeded to this company—at a time when, as Robert Heilbroner ironically notes, the federal government was busy *selling* land to small homesteaders. The railroad builders, not content with federal assistance, threatened to bypass small communities along the right-of-way until they donated cash and property, and persuaded the San Francisco city fathers to give them $1 million. The California state government was also among the donors to their enterprise.[17]

Since the advent of federal regulation of business (much of which was necessitated, of course, by its collapse in 1929), entrepreneurial practices have not been so flamboyant as those of a century ago. But there are still strange inconsistencies about a businessman who publicly avows adherence to competition, individualism, and free trade, while privately exerting every effort to secure government subsidies, to fix prices, and generally to reduce the very risks he supposedly embraces. Such massive government assistance programs as the oil depletion allowance or airline subsidies or the granting of monopoly rights to utility companies are justified, like the railroad acts of years before, on the grounds of pressing public interest. Similarly, tax writeoffs which benefit individuals, such as donations to cultural or charitable institutions, are allowed because such gifts also benefit the public. But, although much has been accomplished through social programs, increased public support for the aged, the poor or the ill is still frequently denounced as antithetical to American faith in free enterprise.

Particularly curious are the contradictory stances which have been taken regarding the schools. In the main, education has been recognized as a public responsibility, an essential component of a democratic society, and the chief means (along with virtue) whereby even the poor could hope to rise to eminence and wealth. From colonial and pioneer days, from the establishment of universal public education at elementary and secondary levels to the founding of private or public institutions of higher education (particularly the land-grant colleges), Americans have paid glowing tribute to the power of education. Over and over the same themes appeared: only through education for all Americans could the wilderness be tamed, the republic be governed well, economic progress be ensured, and the heterogeneous citizenry be unified. And as America steadily expanded in size, in population, and in wealth, its progress was taken as visible evidence of the success of the schools and a justification of their cost.[18]

But from time to time education has suddenly been found to have limitations on what it could accomplish. Perhaps, after all, there were some individuals or groups who were simply incapable of profiting from education. During Reconstruction, for example, many voices were raised to protest the establishment of common schools for the newly-freed slaves or, at least, to suggest that their curriculum be strictly limited to "practical" subjects. Daniel H. Chamberlain, a Yankee who served as the Republican attorney general and later governor of South Carolina during Reconstruction, lived to have second thoughts about the wisdom of some radical Republican and abolitionist policies, especially those advocating extensive education for freedmen. In an article for the 1901 *Atlantic Monthly,* he wrote this:

> (The negro) does not need . . . higher education . . . (A) great amount of money and effort has been worse than wasted on such education, or attempts at such education, of the negro. To an appreciable extent, it has been a positive evil to him. Give him, or rather stimulate him to provide himself, education suited to his condition: to wit, abundant training in the three R's; and after that skill in handicraft, in simple manual labor of all kinds, which it is his lot to do—lot fixed not by us, but by powers above us . . . (L)et the negro be taught . . . thrift, pecuniary prudence and foresight . . .[19]

The arrival, around the turn of the century, of thousands upon thousands of poor immigrants created new challenges for public education. Once again, the schools were looked to as the institutions which could indoctrinate the newcomers in the American language and traditions and start them up the ladder of success. Colin Greer, in *The Great School Legend,* describes how the almost mystical faith in the schools as the "melting pot" of American society gradually hardened into a conviction that they were in fact responsible for "solving" the immigrant problem. When, occasionally, evidence came to light that not all immigrants *had* moved successfully into the mainstream, it was impossible to believe that the schools had failed.[20] Greer explains:

> Since, as it appeared, the schools were capable of creating mobility for some of the poor, for those who seemed 'willing to take advantage of the opportunities offered them,' then it seemed to follow that there was something inherently wrong with those ethnic groups which were not succeeding in the school or afterward. Clearly, the fault was not to be placed with the schools. Increasingly, ethnic, genetic, and racial hypotheses were advanced to explain away the failure of some of the poor. The first victims of these theories were the Irish and the Italians; then, when poor blacks displaced poor immigrants as the majority of the urban school population, they inherited the honor of being the unteachable element in what would otherwise be an efficient and successful school system.[21]

The 1960s, however, saw widespread renewal of the old faith in education as the crucial means for making the nation great. The decade's extraordinary efforts to improve American schools were sparked in part by the shock of Russian success in space science, and in part by the implications of the 1954 *Brown* decision that "separate facilities are inherently unequal." The nation was forced to reexamine its school systems and repair their weaknesses, both as a matter of self-defense and in order to comply with the Constitution. Longstanding opposition to federal involvement in education (which had always been regarded, legally and emotionally, as a local or state concern) crumbled, as Congress passed measures designed to aid the nation's schools.

One innovation after another was launched with new assertions of the achievements which would be made, for all and by all, now that the schools had both adequate funding and unlimited freedom to experiment with new curricula and methods.

But the hoped-for progress was not made, certainly not on the scale once imagined. Despite the ferment, reform efforts, and federal funds, school systems, particularly in the urban areas which had been a special target for new programs, were just about the same. Inevitably, disillusionment and anger—that so much effort and expense had achieved so little—set in; just as inevitably, voices were soon repeating the old refrains: "You expected too much of the schools and anyway some people are just ineducable." What had been said at earlier junctures was being said again: if the schools cannot successfully transform the urban poor into productive workers (or slaves into independent citizens, or immigrants into "good Americans"), the explanation is to be found, not in the schools, but in those groups' basic (and probably innate) deficiencies.

JENCKS ON INEQUALITY

By far the best-publicized recent attack on unlimited faith in education, even "reformed" education, is that made by Christopher Jencks. "None of the evidence we have reviewed," writes Jencks, "suggests that school reform can be expected to bring about significant social changes outside the schools. More specifically, the evidence suggests that equalizing educational opportunity would do very little to make adults more equal."[22]

The findings of Jencks and his associates were published in late 1972 as *Inequality: A Reassessment of the Effect of Family and Schooling in America*. The book, carrying with it the prestige of Harvard-M.I.T. (where the book was developed and written) and of the Carnegie and Guggenheim foundations (which largely funded the research and writing), has been readily adopted by those who are looking for reasons to tear down or abandon altogether the Great Society's emphasis on securing equality of opportunity through improving the schools. Jencks himself (who is very much in favor of reducing inequality) was not only aware, but irritated by, the unseemly speed with which his work was being picked up by opponents of educational change or improvement, as he indicated shortly after *Inequality* appeared:

> Some people are now using our conclusions to justify limiting educational expenditures and abandoning efforts at desegregation . . . Politicians and school boards . . . have seized on our research to justify what they want to do anyway . . . (I)t does not follow that we should sweep the problems under the rug, or use the fig leaf of social science to claim that they are not important.[23]

The fact remains, however, that the intent of his book is clearly (as its jacket indicates) to "challenge much of contemporary social policy" and to demonstrate (among other things) that "school quality has little effect on achievement or economic success." What could be more logical than to conclude that institutions which are so obviously not doing what they were thought to be doing are hardly worth the enormous amounts of time, money, and energy which have been expended in their behalf? What else could be made of such statements as these?

—Economic success seems to depend on varieties of luck and on-the-job competence that are only moderately related to family background, schooling, or scores on standardized tests.[24]

—Adequate school funding cannot, then, be justified on the grounds that it makes life better in the hereafter.[25]

—Thus, we cannot expect universal preschooling to narrow the gap between rich and poor or between whites and blacks.[26]

—No measurable school resource or policy shows a consistent relationship to schools' effectiveness in boosting student achievement . . . (and) the gains associated with any given resource are almost always small.[27]

—Qualitative differences between high schools seem to explain about two percent of the variation in students' educational attainment.[28]

—The evidence we have reviewed suggests, however, that the long-term effects of segregation on individual students are quite small.[29]

—Our research suggests, however, that the character of a school's output depends largely on a single input, namely the characteristics of the entering children. Everything else—the school budget, its policies, the characteristics of the teachers—is either secondary or completely irrelevant.[30]

Whether Jencks intended them to or not, such statements clearly imply that improving schools is a waste of time since education has little effect on later achievement. But a further inference can be drawn from his conclusions: if the "characteristics of the entering children" are indeed almost the sole factor in determining educational success (school "output"), obviously educational failure can be explained by deficiencies in the children themselves, rather than in the school. Again what could be more logical than to accept theories, conveniently provided by other scholars, that as a class the poor are unable to "defer gratification" long enough to take advantage of education opportunity, or as a race, blacks are so "genetically inferior" that they will never equal whites in educational achievement.

It is not the purpose of this paper to refute Jencks' findings point by point. That is being done systematically and well by many others, who point, for instance, to his use of poor data and faulty statistical modes and techniques.[31] But to refer to others who are systematically criticising Jencks work is not enough. It is possible, in these few pages to sketch the outline of some of the major criticisms.

Alice Rivlin notes, correctly I think, that Jencks work should be viewed as forensic social science; that is, not a part of the tradition of social scientists who hide or claim to hide their personal biases and attempt to present all of the arguments on both sides of a set of questions so that the reader may judge for himself. Rather this work is representative of what may be a new tradition where a scholar or team of scholars take on the task of writing a brief for or against a particular policy. In this particular treatise, Jencks et al. are concerned with reducing inequality in income, but as Rivlin points out, educational reform is clearly not the most direct way to approach this problem. To illustrate this point, $100 billion or 40 percent of the national budget is directed toward income support or redistribution of income: social security, food stamps, public assistance, medicare, medicaid, veterans pensions, housing subsidies, and the like. By contrast, if one adds up the money for education of low-income children, (vocational education, Headstart, the Elementary and Secondary Education Act and other compensatory programs) the total is about $5 billion or 2 percent of the federal budget. And although it is true that most money for education comes from the state and local governments, this money is not directed toward low-income children but toward the education of all children.[32]

Rivlin goes on to point out that few people have contended that educational reform is a more effective way to reduce inequality of income than giving money to the poor, and Bayard Rustin makes an even more direct attack by pointing out that Jencks poses an all or nothing view and his stated goal is therefore utopian and defeatist. Rustin argues that:

> To accede to such an 'all or nothing' view would be to acknowledge that the principles and goals of the civil rights movement have generated so much wasted motion. And yet the evidence is clear and quantifiable that blacks have made substantial progress in education . . . Such gains cannot be written off as chance. Nor is the progress irrelevant, despite what the counterculturists tell us . . . We are living in a credentials oriented society which exacts harsh penalties for the undereducated.[33]

James Coleman, author of the massive and controversial "Coleman Report," also finds much to question in Jencks study. Coleman argues that Jencks minimizes the importance of family background in educational attainment and the effect of occupational status and income, thereby obscuring the inequality of opportunity which does exist in our society. Coleman also observes that money and consumption are not the source of all satisfaction. But even if one uses income as the only variable, how does one account for the other variations in income: baseball players' salaries, salaries of college professors? Can these be accounted for by education? Varieties of luck? Or are they explainable by such common sense variables as age and time on the job or specific skills such as the ability to steal bases or hit home runs? The most interesting observation made by Coleman, however, may be that we have not studied other skills the way we have studied cognitive attainment. How important, for example, are social skills, entreprenurial skills, or management capability to the level of income one attains? And what is the relationship of education to these skills.[34]

Criticisms of the Jencks conclusions are not hard to locate although they have seldom received the exposure and publicity the original work received in the media. Stephen Michelson argues that Jencks findings represent lifetime income chances for some people but misrepresent those chances for others. Although Michelson did not identify them, they would surely include blacks,

Chicanos, Puerto Ricans, and native Americans.[35] For these groups education has been and continues to be the primary means of moving into the professions and out of poverty into well-paying jobs within one generation. And even though the income differential is pronounced between whites and members of these minority groups with similar educational attainment, the fact remains that education, particularly if it includes a college degree, is a primary means for upward mobility *and* improved income.

Charles Asbury of Howard University was particularly angered by the suggestion that schools do not make a difference.[36] He cites Dentler and Warshauer's study *Big City Dropouts and Illiterates* as evidence of the direct correlation between schooling, jobs, and income.[37] Even more forcefully he argues that the all too frequent instances of school failure can be explained by the faulty theory and implementation of many compensatory education programs. Public education has never been given an opportunity to work. It is ridiculous to pretend that it has had adequate funding or public support, and equally silly to have thought that deep seated school and social problems can be fixed by a hastily conceived series of crash programs tried in the 1960s. Moreover, there have been well-documented violations of the law, both by misapplication of funds and deliberate frustration of desegregation efforts.[38]

And yet, despite these violations and failures in conception and implementation, there have been successes. The Center for Educational Policy Research at Harvard reported positive relationships between resources and achievement.[39] James Guthrie reported seventeen instances of compensatory programs with positive correlations between schooling resource variables and pupil performance.[40] Other examples could be cited. What about the experiences in Upward Bound programs? Sixty-nine to 72 percent of alumni of these programs are in college as compared to 39 to 48 percent of older brothers and sisters.[41]

Henry Levin, a Stanford University economist, summarizes his critique of Jencks by saying:

> The ommision of important variables because of 'ignorance of their effects,' the casual ordering of the variables, assumptions of linear relationships and normal distributions, the scavenging and use of data collected for other purposes and the questionable treatment of their measurement errors, as well as the ambiguity of many of the results, means that the actual findings and interpretations are at least as much a product of *value perspectives* and *opinions* of the researcher as they are of this methodology and data.[42] (emphasis added)

The Jencks study, despite its characterization as forensic social science, does nothing to advance either side of the policy issue and it is the policy issues we should be concerned about at this time in our history. For example, Jencks offers varieties of luck as an explanatory variable without offering any evidence to support this selection. He groups income and earnings together as if they were the same. Yet there is a significant difference between rent, dividends, and capital gains on the one hand and social security, welfare, and wages on the other. An appreciation of these differences would surely alter the proportions of variance in incomes reported in this study. Even more important, no corrections in income were made for region of the country, age, sex, race, hours worked or number of persons in the family contributing to income, variables which are routinely considered in income studies. An even more compelling criticism made by Rivlin is that Jencks fails to expose his data to scholars and lay people. He cites many unpublished sources and his presentation of data contributes little to clarity.[43]

The most serious criticism may be subsumed under questions of public policy. Michelson argues that this book is a good example of how academic papers influence public policymakers and provide rationales for shifts in public policy.[44] Kenneth Clark is even more direct and criticizes publicity as a means of promoting social science findings among non-social scientists who then make decisions influenced by people hawking their wares. Clark observes that social science findings have a greater chance of being well received and publicized when they support present biases. And in the present climate of this country, Jencks contributes to the litany of immobility and despair. He suggests that children are blocked not only by culture and genes, but by essential and inherent meaninglessness of schools. This argument now provides the rationale for policymakers to say there is no need to desegregate, to decentralize schools, to equalize expenditures or, for that matter, to adequately maintain them.[45]

Nowhere does Jencks deal with educational goals of social sensitivity, respect for justice or the acceptance of differences among human beings. Nowhere does he, nor did Coleman before him, probe the attitudes of teachers to see if teachers felt it was the child's fault or the school's fault if a child did not learn, clearly an important question if we give any credence to the concept of the self-fulfilling prophecy. Very little data were gathered and analyzed to see how resources and policies were applied within individual schools as opposed to school systems. Gerald Grant asks the question: Would an upper-class child be placed in a slow learner class as quickly as a poor child?[46]

Perhaps the most devasting criticism comes from Philip Jackson of the University of Chicago who argues that Jencks gives insufficient attention to what education is all about and what schools are trying to do. Never does Jencks admit the possibility that better schools might lead to a better education. Perhaps it is as Jackson says—Jencks is a reformer, not an educator. As a reformer, he takes a relativistic position on education. He never once speaks out for the life enhancing possibilities of education. His conclusions and assertions are a reflection of what exists, not a vision of what could be if fundamental changes were made and given a chance to work.[47]

Finally, it should be repeated that educational research is a primitive art. The methodology and information needed to establish the connection between school characteristics and pupil performance simply do not exist. As Rivlin notes:

> If the world were organized to suit policy analysts this question
> would surely be attacked experimentally. It would be possible to
> take groups of students who had the same family characteristics
> and abilities and give them different educational 'treatments' for
> a sustained period. It would be possible to try out high and low
> budgets, to vary class sizes, curriculum, teaching method, and edu-
> cational philosophies. A basis would then exist for determining
> whether some varieties of education worked better than others.
> Since such experiments have not been done the analysts have been
> forced to make inferences from data generated by the existing
> system. . . . The pooh-poohers of school effectiveness do not stress
> the limitations of the survey data since these data seem to bolster
> their case.[48]

And so one returns to a point made at the beginning of these comments: *why* is the question being raised at this particular juncture? If one understands the context for the question, I think one might see it for what it is worth, suitably ignore it, and spend his energies on the more precise, and more exacting problems which confront the educational community. Let us attempt, then, to sketch that context.

Education has been the focus of the struggle and efforts over the past twenty years—dating from the 1954 *Brown* decision—to rectify racial injustice and to eradicate the blight of poverty in this country. No institution has been the subject of as much criticism, attack, concern, and activity as the public schools: we need not recount here the series of battles over desegregation, curriculum reform, functional illiteracy, community control, innovations of various sorts. The point is that public education has been ordered, by judicial fiat, urged, by concerned citizens, and persuaded, by federal and foundation funds, to changes its ways—and the successive waves of change have left in their wake a residue of discontent, frustration, and resentment; frustration that so little has been accomplished and resentment at the dislocations and expense. We had hoped, like the medieval alchemists, to find the magic potion which would make education golden, and instead we have concocted a witches brew of militancy, anger, and misunderstanding which threaten to destroy public education as we have known it. This hope, however, led to a strange notion: that public schools, particularly in urban areas, were so bankrupt—educationally, financially, and morally—that only massive change imposed from the outside can lead to perceptible improvement or reform. Basic to this notion, however, is the assumption that few if any among the professional staff—teachers, administrators, specialists—are sensitive enough to the dysfunctions of systems of public education to attempt to do anything about it. And even those hardy and courageous individuals who do try to change the system have little, if any, effect. As indicated earlier, we have been told over and over that one good year is not enough.

Upon examination, one finds this notion not only strange, but more than a little upsetting. It seems to be at odds with what appears to be a self-evident reality. First, few outsiders know as well and in as much detail as the insider the strengths and deficiencies of an institution or a system. Such a reality applies as much to education as it does to medicine, law, architecture, engineering, and other professions. The insider is always privy to more information, is more aware of nuances and subtleties of a profession or craft than are those not privy to what sociologists call the secular and sacred objects of the field.[49] Second, the quality of service or product are differentiated. It should be obvious that there are excellent, good, average, and poor physicians, lawyers, social workers, and teachers. Third, it is dangerous and, some would argue, irresponsible to cite generalizations which do not take due account of such important variables as the location, program, nature of service, the period of time in which such service is rendered and, even more important, the internal and external constraints which affect the delivery of such services.

What is often overlooked or, at the very least, seldom mentioned is the fact that there are those who carry out their responsibilities—quietly for the most part, but sometimes not so quietly—doggedly and effectively. These individuals—and they are not so extraordinary either—make a difference. Often, perhaps usually, they make their compromises with the system and do their best. Others confront the system and, in effect, "do their thing" in spite of it. Perhaps most of them merely ignore the constraints—implied or real—understanding that unless a major catastrophe or a total lack of "order and discipline" occur, few, if any, in positions of power will know the difference anyway. The possibilities abound, as students of organization have pointed out, for the individual or the individual school to engage in many activities not formally prescribed. The nature of school systems is such that the units are spread over large geographic areas, individual teachers and administrators operate within the privacy of their schools and classrooms, administrators not only spend relatively little time observing classroom instruction but administrators are themselves very loosely supervised, if at all. The larger the system, the more accurate these observations.[50]

What many of the critics of public education have failed to perceive clearly, in all of its dimensions, are the limited but important improvements and contributions made by individuals and/or programs in schools. One might readily agree with some critics that the humane and creative contributions to the learning process are more notable by their absence than by their presence; they are nonetheless important. And while one good teacher, one good principal, one good school, or one good year may not be enough, they are significant and indeed, for some students, may in fact be enough.

A note of caution and explanation is appropriate: the role of the critic, whether outside or inside the system, is important. Theodore Roosevelt to the contrary, it is the critic who counts. But not to the exclusion of the doers. Views of critics have and do provide an important and needed counterpoint to the self-serving and self-defensive mouthings and posturing of too many educators. Critics have informed an often apathetic and ill informed public about the soft underbelly of public education. They have substantiated for many the uneasy feeling that all is not well in the public schools. But it is also true that, for many young people, exposure to a school, a teacher, a principal, a counselor has made a difference, perhaps the difference in a positive as well as the more often reported negative sense. It might have been possible—it *should* have been possible—to view our half-successes and even our failures with equanimity, to exert that typically American pragmatism which meets disaster philosophically and turns men to devising better schemes even while the debris of disaster is being cleared away. Certainly, not all the programs to improve education were well planned; most were not given enough time to work; none was funded adequately (despite the current rhetoric about the "massive amounts of federal aid which have been poured into education"). But such facts might once have simply been taken as evidence that we needed to work harder at the task. Tragically, too many have taken another road—that of defeatism and despair. Apparently we have decided—we who conquered the wilderness and made the desert bloom and put men on the moon—that some problems are incapable of being solved, that all our billions and our expertise are, at last, helpless when it comes to teaching a poor black or Chicano or Indian child to read or to find a job. A failure of nerve in a formerly fearless man is a sad thing—but it is forgivable, it is understandable, it can be overcome. What is obscene about our present situation is the incredible willingness of many people—encouraged by some of our national leaders—to justify our failures by blaming the victims of them. As if in response to society's basest instincts, the new sorcerers and shamans have stolen into our midst to offer once again theories of genetic inferiority, concepts of a culture of poverty which keeps people from emerging from their self-induced misery, and warnings about the limits on what government can rightfully be expected to accomplish. Contributions from such various fields as psychology, sociology, and political science have been carefully orchestrated into a full-scale "scientific" rationale for the slackening or abandonment of national efforts to redress the grievances of the poor, or the oppressed.[a]

Since education has been the focus of so many of our earlier programs—the Elementary and Secondary Act, the Economic Opportunity Act, to

---

[a]I have examined this phenomenon at greater length in a monograph published by the National Urban Coalition.[51]

name only two—it is hardly surprising that education should be the object of a
key line of attack. Backed by the prestige of academia and foundations, armed
with statistical analyses churned out by his infallible computers, surrounded by
the spotlights of national media coverage, Mr. Jencks has informed us that
schools don't matter. Luck, personality—things we can't do anything about,
by definition—turn out to be the magic ingredients in the formula of success
in life, but the quantity or quality of education to which one is exposed is all
but irrelevant. Need I remind you that we live in a "credential society"? However
narrow or crass a view of education this may seem to entail, it is obvious that a
major objective of each level of education is to prepare students for the next
level. Whatever we may feel about the abuses of the whole complicated system
of credits, certification, and credentials, there is no escaping the reality: Few
are going to get into law school without a baccalaureate degree; few can go on
to college without presenting evidence of having completed high school. In the
face of common sense, philosophy and the accumulated experience of mankind,
here stands Jencks, like others before him, to tell us that all this time we have
been barking up the wrong tree. Schools don't matter. After all, he is a leading
proponent of egalitarianism, and his book was intended as a call to equalizing
income—he just happens to believe that it will not be achieved by improving
educational opportunity. But he and his colleagues cannot escape the responsibility for the "unanticipated consequences" of his work. Clearly, his recent
book has become an integral part of what *Social Policy* accurately called the
"new assault on equality,"[52] one more justification for the current policy of
dismantling many Great Society efforts and cutting back on spending for social
welfare and educational programs. Small wonder that educators, parents, and
concerned citizens, who have lived through years of controversy about the
schools, churned up by militant unions, angry students or such radical thinkers
as Ivan Illich, are now thoroughly confused and disillusioned. Small wonder
that those who have fought and argued and worked to find more equitable ways
to fund our educational system are disheartened to learn from the Supreme
Court that education is not among the rights afforded explicit or implicit protection under the Constitution. Small wonder, after all, that many Americans
gather in conference and living rooms to ponder whether education makes a
difference.

Does education make a difference? Of course it does. There will always be arguments—and there should be—about specific issues connected with
our schools. Some people will always feel that they are expected to do too much,
while others believe that they are not doing enough. Unfortunately, the greatest
danger is not in the argument, but in the temptation to short-circuit it by looking for simplistic analyses and simpler solutions. One example of this kind of
thinking is found among those who profess great interest in studying genetic
inferiority. All too readily, they would write off certain groups as incapable of
profiting from academic education and dictate for them an "easier" curriculum,
one "in keeping" with their abilities.

But this country was founded on and its integrity depends on the profound belief in the worth of each individual and in his right to decide for himself how far and how fast he will move: economically, socially, culturally, and politically. We have already witnessed far too much loss and pain and damage from the frustration and suppression of individual talent. Are we now to hand over the educational decision-making power to those who claim on the basis of science or statistics to "know" what is best for entire segments of the population? I am certainly not ready to do so, given the serious deficiencies of much of educational research, the inescapable bias of much of what is advertised as "objective" or "value-free" findings, the strange correlation between political strategies and social theories.[53]

But perhaps after all, asking the question of whether education makes a difference will serve a useful purpose. Perhaps it will force us to face the inadequate and even disastrous conditions of much of what passes for education in this country. Perhaps it will encourage us to begin defining more precisely just what difference we want education to make. Perhaps it will encourage us to demand, of educators and politicians alike, that we begin in this country to devote to education, particularly basic and elementary education, the same energy and money and determination which helped us conquer the wilderness, win wars, and put a man on the moon.

One can hope that most Americans will refuse to be distracted from what can and ought to be done; will spend no more time discussing a question to which we all know the answer; and will get on with the difficult, demanding, but honorable and essential task of seeing that education *does* make a difference, a worthwhile and satisfying difference, to each of America's children.

Chapter Two

The School as Context

The popular picture of the urban school principal is that of the man in the middle, caught up in a storm of angry and frequently contradictory demands. Beseiged by noisy delegations of students, parents, teachers, or community residents, he finds himself simultaneously to blame for poor facilities, too much homework, insufficient time for faculty planning, and student misconduct on the way to school. When he is finally able to close his office door, he is confronted by a desk full of forms to be filled out and telephone calls to be returned to the district superintendent, the curriculum office, and the personnel department. Should he ever venture from the comparative safety of his building, he is likely to run straight into representatives of the press or the local television station who are eager to record his views on the latest crisis for the evening news audience. Once he might have been the dignified scholar-statesman, presiding over serene classrooms of dutiful pupils. Today he often resembles the unfortunate victim of a pack of avenging furies.

Despite this popular picture, the reality of many schools, urban as well as suburban and rural, may be quite different. Schools exist, in cities as elsewhere, which operate with a degree of calm; faculties and administration perform their functions with a relatively clear notion of goals and objectives. And students, with notable exceptions, attend classes, learn and exercise options with a reasonable degree of satisfaction. More importantly, such schools exist almost side by side and within the same public school system with schools which approximate the popular picture described above. The fact that such a condition could and in fact does prevail is not only unknown to many parents, citizens, and other educators, it would surprise and confuse many of them.

23

One is reminded of an incident which occurred several years ago in one of the largest cities in this country. The city superintendent invited a group of superintendents from surrounding suburban areas to spend two days visiting city schools. Among the schools visited was one which had a reputation for being "tough"; it had been described in the press as a school with a militant and activist student body and an equally active community. At the conclusion of the two-day visit, the visiting suburban superintendents were invited to lunch and during the course of the luncheon several suburban superintendents expressed surprise that they had not witnessed assaults, open displays of weapons, and expressions of surliness and disrespect by students toward teachers. One suburban superintendent observed that this "tough" school compared favorably with the so-called "good" schools he had seen on his visit.

He wondered how such conditions could prevail in a school with this reputation. Perhaps it had something to do with the principal, his faculty, and the context in which that particular school operated. It is true that similar schools within the same public school system might operate quite differently, have a different image and, indeed, have "different goals and objectives." Such differences have always existed and, in fact, may be more obvious and observable today than in the past. It is the leadership and the staff as much as the student body and community which shape and influence the operation and the ultimate product of the school, always within the context of the total system and society. It seems appropriate, therefore, to review some of the pressures which continue to impinge on the role and function of school principals and program directors. An historical perspective may enable us to understand more fully the way principals, teachers, and individual schools have operated and are forced to operate today.

THE PRINCIPAL'S ROLE

The basic organizational pattern of most urban school system has not changed greatly in recent years, despite the publicity given to some scattered experiments with decentralization or community control. There is still a superintendent of schools, who has the overall responsibility for the smooth functioning of the educational system. With him at the central office, there is a complete hierarchy of administrators who may have staff or line functions. In the field, there may be intermediate line officials, district or area superintendents, who supervise the several sub-districts and who, in turn, have their own staff to monitor and advise on specific aspects of the local educational system. The individual student or parent may view a principal as master of all he surveys; the principal is more likely to see himself as the bottom man on a large and imposing totem pole.

Formal constraints are imposed on the prerogatives of the administrative roles by state statutes and the rules of the state department of education, which deal with such matters as the basic curriculum, teacher qualifications, length of the school day and year, and so on.[1] Closer to home, the size of the local operating budget and the various contracts with employee organizations circumscribe all too clearly the area within which the systems' administrators may exercise their judgment in the allocation of funds. While the individual principal's degree of freedom may vary from one system to another, he is generally empowered to modify or add courses, assign personnel within the limits of student enrollment and interest, slect books, materials, and equipment from approved lists, expend varying sums of discretionary monies according to his own priorities, and seek the involvement of parents and other community residents. No doubt the philosophy of his general and district superintendents and the city board of education (whether or not expressed in specific goals and objectives for the system as a whole) will constitute an influence on the principal's decision-making process, as will issues of current concern, e.g., the need for expansion of ethnic studies, the institution of innovative approaches to teaching science, or the interest of local businesses in creating a work-study program.[2]

When all these real and possible constraints are taken into account, however, the fact remains that most large school systems define the formal limits of the principal's authority in only the most general way. Such definitions usually take the form of central office memoranda which are far from specific, except as they relate to the law and to local boards of education regulations and policies. It would not be inaccurate to say that they are intended to avoid controversy or to prevent a recurrence of actions which have led to past controversy; in other words, to protect the board and central administration from embarrassment. Why, then, has the notion of the beleaguered principal—beset, so to speak, behind and before—taken hold of the popular and even professional imagination?

THE PRINCIPAL'S TRAINING

Part of the explanation may be found in the literature on educational administration, which has all too often defined the principal's role in a simplistic way. In the early part of this century, Frederick Taylor and the other exponents of administrative efficiency depicted the principal as a business manager, who needed only to learn and apply the new-found principles of scientific management in order to assure his success.[3] Luther Gulick and Lyndall Urwick, in their formulation of organizational principles, devised POSDCORB (planning, organizing, staffing, directing, coordinating, reporting, and budgeting) as an exhaustive description of an executive's responsibilities.[5] The so-called "human relations movement" in administration, brilliantly exemplified by Mary Parker Follett, added important new insights from psychology and sociology,[5] but in lesser hands these often served merely to soften the cold calculating business manager approach by the addition of some humane and rather paternalistic techniques.

The search for generalizations was far from over, but the field was perhaps too narrow. It remained for Talcott Parsons, Herbert Simon, Jacob Getzels, and others to invent a wider lens, focusing on entire organizations in their social context.[6] Then it was possible to engage in systematic research and analysis, model-building and theoretical work on a base sufficiently broad to take into account the rapidly changing and complex realities of various administrative roles.

It has now become apparent that leaders are not simply born with the ability to lead; but neither are they engineers who can apply a tried and true remedy to each specific problem. They must learn to be conceptualizers, mastering theory in order to use it in understanding the day-to-day demands, while simultaneously modifying their theories with pragmatic experience. It should not be inferred, however, that theories of social organization, political processes or group dynamics are sufficiently sophisticated to explain why and how human beings act as they do. The social sciences are—and may always be—far from exact. Unfortunately, not all prospective principals have been exposed, in their educational administration courses to even the available interdisciplinary insights which might help prepare them to deal with their multifaceted role in a complex organization.

If an urban principal's background is limited to the more traditional knowledge, he is likely to be ill-prepared to handle the new demands and expectations pressing in upon him. Teacher militancy, civil rights agitation, pressure for community involvement or control, student rebellion—all these movements have been creating issues and problems which are scarcely touched on in the conventional wisdom of the schools, and which do not yield to a cookbook approach to management. Compounding the error, some departments of educational administration have not only restricted their students' thinking to POSDCORB type of framework, but they have also led them to believe that a principal's "bag of tricks" is as useful in one setting as in another. They have failed, in other words, to take into consideration, or to convey to their principal candidates, that very different skills, competencies, and understandings may be needed in one setting from those appropriate for another.

Small wonder, then, that many principals feel ill-prepared, ill-used, or both, when confronted by the apparently endless crises facing urban schools. A common complaint among them is that they are blamed for situations which they did not create and which they have no power to ameliorate. The angry parent in the school office to request that a poor teacher be admonished or transferred is not interested in being told of the threat of union intervention. The teacher, in need of aides or supplies or a bus for a trip, doesn't wish to hear the principal repeat that the budget or personnel or order department is holding things up. As far as parents, teachers, and students are concerned, the buck stops on the principal's desk. Yet as one harassed school administrator said: "A few years ago, when there were only 100 employees in the central office, it took four weeks to get the crayons we ordered. Now they have 1,000 people working down there, and we can't even get the requisitions for crayons. I wish I could just go out and buy the damn crayons myself!"

DECENTRALIZATION

Ironically, the moves toward administrative decentralization, conceived as a way of restoring to field administrators authority and resources commensurate with their responsibilities, have in many instances simply increased the pressures upon them. While the need for massive re-training, education, and development for both central and field personnel has been recognized, there has seldom been sufficient time between crises—and never enough money—to carry out even minimal decentralization in an orderly way, calculated to maximize good will and acceptance. (Significantly, however, in at least one system contemplating extensive reorganization, principals were not even represented in the initial planning sessions.) When actual steps are finally taken to decentralize—e.g., transfer of resource personnel from the central office to district offices or school clusters, installation of a PPBS system—many principals view these as at best bureaucratic juggling with little relevance to their own pressing needs or, at worst, the imposition of new tasks which they are poorly equipped to handle. Indeed, that such management innovations as PPBS might comprise more of a threat than a promise was made explicit in such statements as that made by one deputy superintendent for administration "It would be a serious error to conclude that PPBS allows greater freedom. On the contrary." All the accompanying speeches about creating an atmosphere of mutual trust, in which honest failure is to be encouraged rather than penalized, can hardly erase the resulting climate of fear and emergent hostility. The old caveat against pouring new wine into old wineskins was never more pertinent—yet all the sincere efforts to revive and renew the "swineskins" seems uncannily to run afoul of political and financial realities which make impossible the provision of the critical time and funds for careful transition. Even where substantial decentralization has occurred, the effect has been largely to push down to the second and third levels of administration the agonizing problems of stretching pitifully limited resources over ever-increasing needs.

COMMUNITY CONTROL

While some urban systems attempted, with varying degrees of frustration or success, to make running the schools more manageable through organizational shifts, others opted for—or were forced into—the even more hazardous paths of achieving decentralized management through community participation in school operations. The underlying rationale is similar: moving the decision-making process closer to the interface between teacher and pupil in an admirable attempt to turn schools out of their bureaucratic lethargy into the responsive and dynamic institutions they ought to be. Unfortunately, the history of some of these experiments (too well known or too complex to be recounted here) is hardly calculated to persuade the fearful or cautious of their worth. In many circles, Ocean Hill-Brownsville, Adams-Morgan or Woodlawn are words which strike terror or contempt into educators' hearts.[7]

Community control is a topic which has upset teachers and principals all over the country largely because of the widely-publicized New York City controversy of several years ago. The argument, however, should be put in its proper context: that of the American tendency to double-think. When whites and the affluent demand community control, it is regarded as logical, normal and appropriate. Indeed, they seldom need to "demand" it, because they have generally been in control of their schools from the start. But once poor people or minority groups begin to talk about control, blood pressures skyrocket, eyes bulge, and people begin to see some dark and devious plot being concocted by militants and revolutionaries. Derrick Bell of Harvard University Law School has put the issue in perspective.

> The essence of community control, Bell says, is the sense of parents that they can and do influence policy-making in their children's school in ways beneficial to their children. Parents in highly regarded suburban school communities have this sense, and in varying degrees, teachers and administrators in those schools convey an understanding that their job success depends on satisfying not the board or union but the parents whose children are enrolled in the school.[8]

Or as John Smith of Howard University said more succinctly: "White schools are not 'better' because whites are more superior, but because those responsible are required to act responsibly."[9]

Initially, parent groups in a number of cities, aware of the depressing failures of the schools to educate their children, asked only how they could help to improve things. But community involvement has been in too many instances a charade. As Peter Schrag noted in 1967 "there has been no serious effort made to give the local community a determining voice in establishing curricula and in deciding how a school building should be used."[10] Driven to desperation by the bland assurance, meaningless committee work, and subtle (or not so subtle) put-downs, while the evidence accumulated of systematic favoritism for certain schools and planned inferiority for others,[11] parents and concerned citizens began to talk of taking over the schools. Yet even when state legislatures and the courts have taken up their cause, their victories have been hollow. Marilyn Gittell, one of this country's major analysts of educational politics, summed up the problem by saying that "mere election of local boards is not a guarantee of a redistribution of power." She noted that professionals have seen to it that boundaries and election procedures were such as to assure continued control by the old forces; that in any case organized groups—even those such as parochial parents with no direct interest in the public schools—are favored; and that local boards are limited to dealing with "at best minor housekeeping arrangements."[12] Barbara Sizemore's analysis of the Chicago Woodlawn School leads to similar conclusions: "there the community board was simply an advisory group, recommending policies, not controlling much of anything."[13] And in Philadelphia, the Board of Education's two-year efforts to devise (in conjunction with professional and community groups from all over the city) a rational approach to shared decision-making resulted in a report recommending three options for community groups: informal participation; advisory participation, and shared authority and responsibility.[14] To date, however, not one of these options has been picked up, no visible change has occurred, and none is expected. Community control may or may not be a current issue for many principals, but parent involvement is here to stay. In those places where schools have begun to recognize the constructive potential in a strong home-school-community relationships, the payoff in terms of improved student attitudes, behavior and achievement has been measurable. Continuing to mis-educate children while ignoring or patronizing their parents is no longer possible. The explosive mixture of parental frustration, anger, and despair threatens to burst into a raging fire which could destroy public education as it is known today.

NEGATIVE REACTIONS

The setting in which most urban principals must operate, may seem—and perhaps is—sufficiently forbidding to authenticate the description given earlier. Caught in the squeeze between mounting pressure from the clients on one side, and the central administration on the other, many principals have sought to keep peace at any price—including the sacrifice of their professional integrity. Do the students demand academic credit for frivolous experiments? Fine, we must be relevant, you know. Does the community demand a voice in determining the curriculum? Of course, invite the militants in: we can always (1) snow them with pedagogical jargon; (2) blame downtown for not cooperating; or (3) play the martyr. Is the system attempting serious renewal or reform? Quick, learn the new game, mouth the current rhetoric, and proceed up the ladder of career advancement on a newly acquired reputation of insight into contemporary problems.[15] However he decides to play the game, the school for which a principal of this sort has charge will continue to deteriorate. In one, educational, moral, and behavior standards dissolve altogether in the name of student rights, freedom or sentimental weakness. In another, a power struggle between school administrators and self-appointed community spokesmen exhausts all the participants, and students are forgotten altogether. In still another, a flurry of activity, touted as change, earns approving nods, and before anyone catches on to the superficiality and gimmickery, the principal has moved on to a more lucrative position.

Some principals and field administrators have found that the best way to thread their way through the new realities is to develop a power base among their constituents: students, parents, community activists. They have found that, especially in "disadvantaged areas," the advocacy role has served them well in dealing with the central office and board of education, both of which wish to avoid confrontation as much as possible. Still others have used special programs which have demonstrated some improvement in the education of students as a way to insulate themselves from criticism and punitive sanctions. With the ready assistance of the news media, they have acquired a regional or even national reputation as "innovators," and can thus defy even the best-intentioned attempts of the local system to monitor or change the program.[a]

For those principals whose political and public relations skills are not so well honed, still another response is possible: organization. Unable to deal with the new realities, smarting from the real or apparent slurs on their ability, which they perceive in each new central office effort to train, sensitize or make them accountable, some principals have sought the safety of numbers in unions or professional associations. In at least one major city, such an association has won the right to bargain and negotiate directly with the Board of Education for such items as job protection, advertising and bidding for vacancies, salaries, promotion opportunities, etc.[16] This organizational activity is attributable in no small part to the growing urgency of demands from hitherto excluded groups now seeking admittance to administrative and supervisory ranks in education. Affirmative action plans (usually labeled as reverse discrimination or favoritism by those who oppose them), and/or the increased participation of parent and community activists in the process of selecting principals, are correctly interpreted as frontal assaults on the carefully established "rights" of an entrenched and privileged group. This has led to a series of cases, which has cast the professional associations in the not altogether admirable role of opposing in practice what they presumably preach to their students: equality of opportunity for all Americans. In one city, for instance, the proposal to appoint non-white administrators until some semblance of racial parity had been achieved was challenged by the principals' association. The State Commissioner of Education upheld the local board's position.[b]

---

[a]For example, the Philadelphia Parkway School Program was being studied and widely imitated before it had worked out its growing pains.

[b]On August 27, 1968, the Newark School Board decided to change its eligibility criteria for principals. What they did was to automatically consider those principals who were qualified by credentials and experience. Each principal was required to have an oral interview and a screening committee, which included administrators and the National Teacher Association, looking over the principals' credentials. Those principals who were qualified were put into a pool and out of this pool principals would be chosen; however, principals who were on the eligibility lists under the old system were automatically put into the pool.

Those principals who were on the old system eligibility lists challenged this decision of the board and the matter was referred to the state commissioner. The state

Still another form of reaction to the new realities has been the politicizing of many principals. Educational administrators—like their colleagues on the bench—have never been quite so apolitical as American mythology would indicate.[17] But educational ideology has promoted, and the public has subscribed to, the notions of autonomy and insulation for school administrators in the name of localism, unique service, and professional expertise. More recently, however, the threats to their prestige and to their jobs have motivated some principals to engage in overt political behavior, such as cultivating city councilmen or other political leaders who support their point of view. Ethnic and racial organizations—Italian, Jewish, and black, for example—have been established by educators to provide a power base and a protection from the incursions of competing groups.[18] The politicizing of educators has its corollary in the invasion of the supposedly sacrosanct school system by politicians seeking to use it as a source of patronage and power. Given the size of urban school payrolls, construction programs, and budget for supplies and equipment, this should hardly be surprising. Rather than reacting with shock and horror to these developments, however, educators might well encourage the demythologizing of their profession and eagerly support the renewed recognition that education is a matter of gravest political significance and concern. The great classic treatises on the state—beginning with Aristotle's *Politics* or Plato's *Republic*—devote many pages to education. In more recent times, the work of such eminent scholars as Mannheim, Durkheim, and Weber, to name but a few, clearly indicates the integral relationship between education and the social milieu.[19] The notion that politics and education could be separated, that schools should and could somehow exist "uncontaminated" by politics, is a relatively recent aberration. The developments which are currently forcing education matters into the political arena may succeed only in making the schools pawns in endless power plays. But there is a chance, just a chance, that the questions revolving around the education of future citizens may, as a result of the charges and countercharges of competing interests, recover their rightful importance on the public agenda.

POSITIVE REACTIONS

There is, however, another approach to the principal's job. Instead of reacting to the indubitable difficulties with resentment, panic or attempts to be all things to all men, some men and women have viewed them as exciting challenges. Using their relative autonomy and what Bidwell called the "structural looseness"

---

commissioner referred the issue to the State Board of Education for a decision. The State Board of Education sent the appeal back to the commissioner and told him that a decision had to be reached within thirty days. The commissioner upheld the School Board's action to change their eligibility criteria and procedures and he rendered that decision in October 1968.

of the school system,[20] they have learned to operate in ways which may at first seem to have little to do with the traditional role of the principal or the formal definition of his job as prescribed by the system. While their colleagues are still earnestly seeking for the correct policy, the safe approach, and the guaranteed techniques, these principals devote their energies and time to seeing that their teachers are teaching and their students learning. Their context may be the same school system; their problems identical to those faced by all urban principals. But if they must, they will act in spite of the system; they accept problems, not as unusual or undeserved phenomena, but as part and parcel of the job which they have chosen to do. These people are human, not superhuman, they, too, suffer from exhaustion and failure and weakness. But instead of focusing on their limited resources and abilities, or searching for other people to blame for the deplorable conditions under which they work, these people seem almost to thrive on impossible situations.[21] Some have been identified and honored for their work; others continue to plug away in relative obscurity. But here and there across the nation, word continues to filter out that amid the confusion and complexity of the urban principalship, creative and flexible people are redefining the role of the principal in a way which commands respect and replication. What are the characteristics, so far as they can be gleaned from the sparse and scattered accounts, of successful urban principals? If they were to get together and compile a list of operating instructions, it might look something like this.

First, the principal has to take stock of his situation. To indicate that he must know where he is before he can determine where to go may seem painfully obvious. But unfortunately, like other basic common-sense propositions, it is more often honored in the breech than in the observance. Analyzing strengths and weaknesses, identifying resources and needs, is the essential first step. "Taking stock" is, of course, a term lifted from the business world: it means counting the inventory, making a list of what is on hand and what is missing. One of the most widely publicized innovative ventures in the country, the Parkway School, was born in just such a moment of inventory. The Director of Development for the Philadelphia[22] system was reviewing a familiar dilemma: more high school space needed, yet money limited and land hard to find. As it happened, his office looked out on several of the city's major cultural institutions—the Art Museum, the Franklin (science) Institute, the public library. "Why couldn't those grand facilities be put to use during the school day, when not many people are free to visit them," he thought to himself—and not too many months later, the School Without Walls was a reality. Not many principals' offices are across the street from art museums, nor will their pressing needs be met in such an unusual moment of illumination. But the lesson to be drawn from the Parkway story underlines the importance of initial and continuing assessment of current needs *and* possible resources, even unlikely or untried resources.

Secondly, the urban principal must determine to deal with the school's most pressing problem, whether or not it appears to be an "educational" one. The late Marcus Foster, whose success in changing both the image and the reality of a high school whose faculty and students had given up won him the prestigious Philadelphia award, had little patience with educators who bemoan the failure of others to ameliorate the conditions of their students' lives. Whatever problems are preventing students from learning—be they medical or nutritional or housing or clothing problems—*are* educational problems, and must therefore be regarded as educators' problems. To think otherwise, said Foster, "not only removes from the teacher (and the principal) the blame for our educational failures . . . it also robs the educator of the initiative for getting things moving."[23] After all, the "experts" in other fields may never solve the problems, or new ones may materialize overnight. Certainly other professional individuals and agencies have a responsibility for seeing to the health and welfare of the young, but the principal can't afford to wait until "they" do the job. He must be prepared and willing to bargain, beg or borrow what his youngsters or his school require to enable the teaching-learning process to go forward. Perhaps curriculum reform or some other project dear to the principal's heart may have to be delayed, while the ingenuity and energy of his staff is turned to tackling more urgent needs.

There are many ramifications of the common—though often inchoate—view of education as something restricted to cognitive development, the filling of empty heads with facts, or a job done in an artificial—not "real life"—setting called school. The same narrow mentality attempts to divorce education from politics, insulate the school from the community, and remove controversy from the classroom. Curiously enough, the constricted definition belongs not only to "traditional" educators, but colors the thinking of even the most devastating critics of public education. Rarely does one find any reference to the deeper crises in the larger society: unemployment, war, political power, hunger, and pollution.

Similarly, the principal who is not concerned about the willing to take on the crises outside his classroom may be the most fatally irrelevant item in the school inventory. Dr. Foster's program will not fit all school administrators: it was not intended to serve as a prescription, simply description. But his philosophy—that principals should find out what is hurting most and fix that first—is a healthy antidote to the poisonous effects of defining educational responsibilities too narrowly.

A theme which appears again and again in stories of successful school administration is that of willingness to consider the conventional wisdom, and, if necessary, discard it. This is not to be confused with peremptory dismissal of all that has been done in the past—a naive and misleading attitude which has gained a certain radical chic appeal among some younger members of the educational professions. On the contrary, there is much to learn from careful study of the problems faced and the solutions attempted by an earlier generation. (One thinks, for instance, of Waller's *Sociology of Teaching,* written more than forty years ago.[24]) But one must be careful not to mistake the merely conventional ("We've always done it that way") for truly timeless insights.

One principal, well-known for the variety of interesting programs in her school, explained her strategy this way:

> Most administrators go to someone higher up to get permission to do something new, the guy up the line knows that if he approves the program and it doesn't work, he will be blamed for the failure—so as likely as not he'll play it safe and say no. But in this school, we try something out quietly. If it flops, we scrap it. But if it seems to be going well, and we want to expand it, then I march down to my area superintendent and announce that we have a successful program going and we want him to know about it. Of course, I come back with official approval—what else can the superintendent do?[25]

In another school, it became obvious that more time was needed for teacher planning and staff development to work out the details of a recently installed innovative approach. After much discussion, the principal was able to convince the school authorities that the loss of class time from dismissing the students early several times a month would more than be repaid by the higher quality of teacher preparation for the time spent with pupils. In still another school, attended largely by boys already labeled as misfits and delinquents, a new principal quickly became aware of the students' painfully limited exposure to art and music. A fresh supply of books, records, and pictures was helpful, but convinced that these were not sufficient to catch the imagination of her boys, she decided to purchase season tickets to the Friday afternoon concert series of the renowned local orchestra. Staff members and colleagues were horrified at the idea of mixing a busload of unruly youngsters with the staid, white-haired matrons who comprised the concert audience. But she persisted, and the boys' pride, enthusiasm and excellent behavior confused the doubting souls who had envisioned riots in the aisles.

These few examples—many more are possible—should serve to illustrate the point that principals can and do function creatively in spite of the constraints and limited resources imposed by the larger system. This type of administrator recognizes that his chief, perhaps his only job is to design and implement programs which will improve the learning of the children, and which will respond realistically to the aspirations and desires of their parents and the community. He tends to be convinced that rules and regulations are useful only when they are relevant to the social context in which he operates. With refreshing candor, he is likely to admit that the "system" so feared or hated by many lower echelon administrators is largely a myth. When challenged by those with common sense and a humorous perspective, its threatening powers tend to dissolve, like the Wizard of Oz, to fairly ordinary and manageable proportions. Freed from illusions about the oppressive nature of the school hierarchy, and having shaken off the restrictive traditional definitions of his role, the principal is able to undertake the critical task of assessment, and to marshall school and community forces to deal with the real needs of his student body. The particulars of each situation—student performance, teacher abilities, neighborhood resources—will determine his agenda. But while programs may differ, accountability for the product is a universal.

Richard Saxe has stated that "none of the theories and certainly none of the principles based upon experience in other institutions is adequate to explain all the phenomena of the principalship. All of the previous theoretical and experimental data combined are not sufficient for this purpose."[26] But, far from being discouraged, Saxe suggests that there is much available in the literature to aid principals. It is his task to determine the relevance of the data supplied.

Today's urban school presents a unique challenge to an administrator's ingenuity, energy, and patience. He must wear many hats, draw on many sources for wisdom and inspiration. He must be analyst, strategist, and diplomat. But with commitment to his task of making and maintaining an environment in which teaching and learning can flourish, he may discover on the one hand that the system can be made to work, or on the other that his school can work in spite of the system.

Chapter Three

Jim

The principal of Central High School in Stackton was carrying a gun—a 38 Smith and Wesson with a six-inch barrel that bulged in the pocket of his overcoat. His wife and two children had been sent out of town to stay with relatives, away from danger, and his home was being patrolled nightly by police and friends. It was February 1965, and Jim Barns was in the center of a controversy that had Stackton polarized into two opposing factions, facing off in one of the first rounds of a power contest for which the ultimate prize was political control of the city of Stackton itself. It had its beginnings in a simple memo from a principal to his faculty. Another decade or another city, another group of people or another school from that in which Barns found himself and there may have been no crisis, no showdown in a public forum, no threats on his life. But, when Jim began to tighten his administrative control over Central as part of the strategy in a fight to salvage a slum school, he shorted a circuit in a network of power that extended far beyond Central itself. Initially a school issue, Jim Barns confrontation with a faculty member exploded into a major struggle between nascent, grass-roots political activism that had been fragmented, untested, and undirected, and a hulking, corrupt, and brutal—but defiantly effective—political machine that had held Stackton in its grip for thirty-five years. It was a struggle between the demands of the new black consciousness and the power monopoly of the white machine.

That machine was an imposing fortress of power in Stackton until it was partially dismantled by the grass-roots movement in the mayoral election of 1967 won by a black attorney and councilman. Until then, the city of Stackton and Iron County were the private dominion of party bosses and a legion of political appointees who were adept at transforming public power into private wealth. So complete was its control and so domineering was its presence that, prior to the sixties, the machine had all but suffocated the opposition and bankrupted the voting public of any hope of changing the status quo, even though corruption in public office was as blatant as it was widespread. In 1961, the then major of Stackton, was sent to federal prison for failure to report on his federal income tax returns $260,000 he received from kickbacks on city contracts. Several councilmen and other city officials had also been indicted. The machine remained in control, using whatever tactics necessary or profitable. The party membership was drawn from the vast variety of ethnic groups—Greeks, Poles, Hungarians, Armenians, and Italians, among others—who had settled in Stackton to work in the factories, oil refineries, and steel mills. Many of the party members also belonged to a clannish organization founded thirty years before this era. The Diamond Club was as powerful as its companion political party and had itself launched the mayor, several councilmen, and a number of Iron County officials on successful political careers.

The counterforce to Stackton's white political machine was the steady growth and eventual political mobilization of the city's black and Latin population, which, by 1968, would more than comprise 54 percent of Stackton's total citizenry. By the mid-sixties, heightened black consciousness had begun to restructure the attitudes and framework of the political power struggles and was becoming an essential element in the Stackton struggle between machine and populace.

Jim Barnes stepped into the middle of this growing conflict when he was appointed principal of Central High School in 1964. And Central was no prize. The school and the surrounding neighborhood had been the first stop for immigrants who had come to Stackton to work the factories. Over the years, Central had changed from a kindergarten through twelfth grade unit school to a 7-12 school and from white to black as the blue-collar whites moved to other sections of the city where FHA-financed, single-family homes were being built. During the transition period, the separatism and racial conflicts had left their mark on the school. In 1945, as the number of blacks and Mexican-Americans attending the school increased rapidly, there was a strike by white students, led by a young man who was himself a newcomer from Europe, protesting the pressure of large numbers of black students in the school. Much bitterness was engendered by the strike, which kept the school and the city in turmoil for several weeks. Until the fifties, even though the student body was desegregated, social activities, the student government, and some athletic activities remained rigidly segregated. For most of its history, the entire administration, teaching, and supplementary staff had been white, even when the student body became predominately black. And, as political appointees of the local political machine, the school board itself remained all white until 1960.

As Central's neighborhood became increasingly black it also became increasingly poor, the poorest section in the city of Stackton with the lowest

average family income and the largest number of dwellings substandard and un-
fit for human habitation. The Central neighborhood was a slum: the boundaries
of the school included about 90 percent of the narcotics traffic, the highest
incidence of prostitution in the city, and the highest percentage of dropouts.
Wineheads, drug addicts, truants, and dropouts used the school lawn as their
private park, and the old school building itself, badly in need of repair and repainting, blended in with the neighborhood's decay.

If Central had become just another part of the community's problem, and, as such, was increasingly less effective in salvaging the young members
of its community, it had nevertheless been serving other citizens of Stackton.
Until 1969, a succession of white principals had used the school as a stepping
stone to higher positions within and outside the system. The last white principal,
Fondy, who had served at Central from 1956-1960, was Superintendent of
Schools in Stackton when Barns became principal at the high school. This fact
would work against Barns when he faced the crisis at Central.

By 1960, when the student body had become more than 90 percent
black and Spanish-speaking, Central got its first black principal, but no real
change in the effectiveness of its administration. A bright man, well educated,
with a good background and extensive experience prior to arriving at Central,
Dr. Johnson was, nevertheless, not suited to the challenges at the Stackton
school. He had been brought in to the Stackton system from the dual system
in the South, and his administrative style lacked the muscle and the aggressive-
ness that solutions to the black problems of the sixties demanded.

Jim Barns, on the other hand, was a mover and a reformer; a decisive, outspoken, arrogant, and courageous fighter whose force sprang from
and drew on the new consciousness of identity and rights and the new impa-
tience for justice that was part of the civil rights movement of the sixties. His
background prior to Central included a varied and impressive list of professional
achievements: Ph.D. in political science, teaching experience on every level of
education from elementary school to college, and three years as assistant principal in the largest junior high school in Stackton. During his graduate education
he had directed the recreation program in the university's city, and, while attending high school and college, he had been a varsity football and basketball
player, a student leader and a debater. At 6'4", and weighing 200 pounds, Jim
Barns' physical stature as well as his personality and attitude presented an
impressive profile of strength.

Jim had made no secret of the fact that he intended to move Central
off center and start it on a program of reform and renovation. It was also quite
clear that Jim had no intention of being a "yes-man" to the conservative school
board and superintendent. Before he had accepted the position at Central,
through a lengthy series of negotiations and discussions, Barns had demanded
and received the promise of support from the superintendent's office for Central's reform. Painting, renovation, additional permanent staff, and backing for

new programs were all pledged by the Stackton administration before Barns would accept the position. But even with the promised support from the school bosses, the job that Barns faced was a formidable one. Once considered a good school, Central had sent a number of its graduates on to college and political and professional careers, even though the majority of its students generally found their way to the open hearths, blast furnaces, coke plants, and oil refineries in the industrial complex surrounding Stackton. The more black and poor Central became—and by 1964 the student body was 99 percnet black with a few Spanish-speaking students—the smaller the number of graduates going on to college, the greater the number of dropouts, and the greater the decline of academic standards. Discipline and a sense of direction were foreign elements in a student body which had earned a reputation in the community for being rude, surly, unkempt, and generally uncivil. But Central had its own source of morale.

The school may have been decrepit, the cafeteria a small, dirty obscenity, the lawn littered with the wasting of human lives, but when the Central Tigercats strode on to the basketball court, it was with the pride and dignity of a championship team and in a sport that, even on the high school level, was big business and big news in this state. Interest in the Tigercats was not at all confined to the students of Central. Alumni, politicians, syndicate gamblers, and Stackton citizens in general all followed, supported, and attended the high school games, and the pitch of excitement by tournament time was as intense and preoccupying for Stackton citizens as is the Super Bowl for football fanatics and the World Series for baseball fans.

As important to the school as athletics were, however, they had a negative aspect as well. More from the process of academic decline than from that of athletic success, Central was, nevertheless, gradually turning into an athletic mill. Consequently, one of Jim's prime considerations for Central in his first year there was to stress teaching and learning and reestablish the academic side of the curriculum. It was a mammoth undertaking and one which would demand of Barns a number of power plays that would effectively bring the total educational program under his control. To this end, Barns worked to streamline the administrative organization and to consult closely with department heads and teachers on the educational programs. And, because the principal of a school is held responsible for all expenditures and disbursements of funds from whatever source in his school, Jim moved to bring the budget operations of all Central departments in line with administrative approval. And this was when all hell broke loose.

Jim's move on the budget issue had hit a key nerve in the athletic department that set off the reaction and with it, the city-wide controversy. The center of the turmoil was Edward (Buzz) Karniak, physical education teacher and head coach of the Central basketball team for thirteen years and a popular figure in the larger community as well as in the school itself. Unchallenged by previous principals, Karniak had built his own empire at Central. He had become a law unto himself, literally running the athletic department, although technically he was subordinate to the athletic director, and overseeing, without counter-approval from the administration, the expenditure of thousands of dollars each year for department operations. No one had dared cross Karniak. His winning teams were known throughout the state and, in February 1965, his Central Tigercats riding on a 9 and 0 record with three games left in the season, appeared to be on their way to a second consecutive North-West Conference championship.

But, on February 1, 1965, Barns dispatched a memo to the athletic department which said, in effect, that the coaches should seek the approval of the principal before purchasing supplies until such time as the coaches and the principal could jointly work out a new budget procedure. Two days later, without consulting with principal Barns or Superintendent of Schools Fondy, Karniak sent to Stackton newspapers a letter announcing his resignation as basketball coach, effective the end of the school year and his request for a transfer to another school. Usually resignations were announced at the end of the school year and treated, as were other transfers, as routine matters. Karniak, with his autonomy challenged and his team riding the crest of a victorious season, opted for this immediate and public showdown with Jim.

The letter hit like a bombshell: the local daily paper headlined the resignation, sports editors gave it wide coverage, and radio commentators analyzed and speculated on the surprising development. The community began to draw its battle lines and the full dimension of the struggle began to emerge. In addition to his popularity as a coach, Karniak was well-connected politically. He was friendly not only with the mayor of Stackton, but also with the party leadership that ran the local political machine as well as with members of the Diamond Club. And he had powerful friends among the press corps. Karniak's following rallied to his defense in the initial media reports that profiled the coach as an outstanding high school and college athlete, a veteran bomber pilot in World War II, and a successful football, basketball, and track coach. Barns received short shrift in these reports with implications that he was a power-hungry intellectual. Beneath the overt controversy between Karniak's autonomy and Barns' administrative prerogatives lay the covert struggle between the black principal and the white coach with the formidable clout of the political machine behind him.

With the excitement of the basketball season intensifying public reaction and demands for explanations and resolutions bombarding the school board, the Superintendent of Schools, Dr. Fondy, called a meeting for February 4, between Karniak, Barns, the school system's athletic director and the system's supervisor of health, physical education, and recreation. Karniak was asked by Dr. Fondy at this meeting to reconsider, at the end of the current season, his decision to resign as head basketball coach. Karniak gave no definite decision but said he would think about the suggestion. After much discussion, the meeting was adjourned without any resolution to the problem. The failure of the meeting on the fourth was illustrative of the tendency of top school administrators to avoid rather than confront decision; and this was particularly true of Fondy. A former principal at Central, Fondy had administered the school as a caretaker and avoided any controversy. Nor did Fondy's paternalistic attitude toward blacks make him well-suited to deal with the aggressive pride and behavior of a Jim Barns. Fondy's failures to take immediate action and cap the growing eruption of public outrage exacerbated the crisis and encouraged interest groups to take matters into their own hands.

The very next day, actions by supposed Karniak supporters further aggravated the problem and propelled Barns into drastic action. By 3:00 on the afternoon of February 5, a student demonstration was in full swing at Central High School. The demonstrators, some with signs saying "Down with the principal" and "We want our coach" marched through the hall chanting anti-Barns slogans. The protest was quickly broken up by members of the faculty and the students returned to their classrooms, but there were some questions about the demonstration that went unanswered for several days. For one, a local radio station had carried news of a student protest at Central as early as 12:30 on February 5, when the demonstration did not begin until much later that afternoon. Secondly, the signs the students carried were professionally lettered which hinted at the possibility that this was more than a spontaneous, student-engineered act.

Whatever its source and however brief its moment, the protest did get press coverage, and, more profoundly, it did prompt Jim Barns to review the full scope of his problems at Central and assess his position in the current crisis. The promises of financial and administrative support extracted from the central administration before he had signed on as principal had not been forthcoming. Requests from Central High School had been put off by the central administration with excuses about lack of funds and other budget problems. By December, it had become obvious to Jim that the promised support would *never* be forthcoming and, on the twenty-second of that month, he had submitted his resignation in a confidential letter to Superintendent Fondy in which he requested to be reassigned as of January 22 as a teacher in high school social studies or in the upper elementary grades. Fondy refused to act on the resignation and persuaded Barns to remain as principal. None of this exchange had, to this time, been made public. The failure of the central administration to support Barns in the Karniak incident was the last straw for the principal. Unless Jim had that support, there was no way he could reform Central and nothing—not a hefty principal's salary or the prestige of an administrative position—could keep Barns in a position where he had to bargain away the welfare and rights of his students in order to placate the interests of a white power block. For Jim, the days of compromise were at an end.

The struggle with Karniak, significant enough within the dimensions of the question of financial control and school power politics, also touched on and threatened the success of Barns' educational policies for Central, which viewed the strong emphasis on basketball and other sports in the school as an unhealthy one. Technically, Karniak was an instructor in physical education and driver training, but there was little of either being taught while Karniak spent most of his time as well as much of the money allotted to the athletic department on the basketball team. If Karniak was allowed to retain his unquestionable power, Barns would have lost a critical battle in his effort for reform. Another factor, presumed rather than acknowledged openly, intruded upon any possibility for central administration voluntarily supporting Barns' reforms. The more long-standing administrative problems such as the athletic spending that Barns exposed at Central, the more embarrassing it would be for Superintendent Fondy, since it would be clear that Fondy, as a former principal of Central, had been either ignorant or tolerant of these irregularities or ineffectual in their reform. None of the choices presented a pleasant addition to Fondy's reputation.

So in the later afternoon of the same day as the student demonstration, February 5, Jim Barns turned on the public address system at Central and informed the staff and students of his resignation in December and of his current intention to make that resignation final by sending a second letter to the superintendent advising him to take immediate action to relieve him of his duties. Again Barns repeated his offer to accept a non-administrative position, thus underscoring his refusal to compromise the issue in order to remain in power and demonstrating that his resignation was not a self-serving act. Barns would be principal with the rightful powers and support that that position merited or he would not be principal at all. The letter was dictated that afternoon and this time copies of both the first and second letters of resignation were also sent to the president of the school board. Meanwhile, reports of Barns' resignation spread quickly throughout the Central community as excited students brought the news home to their parents.

Now it was the turn of Barns' backers to step into the fray. The fact that they rallied at all was largely owing to Barns' groundwork in the first semester of his administration and to the growing spirit of black activism. Barn's insistence on discipline and pride at Central had struck a responsive chord in the community. He had invited Central parents to join him in his reform efforts and had demanded that they produce; and, for the first time in many years, the Central High School community began to take pride in its school. His spirit and determination had attracted to the Central PTA a new group of activists, many of them middle-class parents from the fringe of Central's catchment area, who would, in the future, become leaders in the poverty programs and movers in community organizations and political activities. Also responding to the dynamism of Jim's leadership was a group of Central Alumni—the Central

Athletic Boosters—who had attended the school under the old style leadership during the days of the previous administrations and the segregation of many of the school's activities. Before Barns, these graduates had felt no real affiliation with the school because of their own limited participation in the school during their student days. Now, with Jim as principal, they saw a black school and a black pride that they could identify with and support. Thus, the Central Athletic Boosters (C.A.B.) came into existence as a direct response to Jim's leadership, and would support him—would, in fact, be his bodyguards—during the Karniak affair.

None of this community action had been effectively operant before the February crisis, but the resignation of Barns galvanized the community into action and produced, on February 6, a team of parents appointed by the Central High School PTA to conduct an independent investigation of the entire incident and a promise to use their influence to solve the current crisis. The investigation, which was based on interviews with both students and teachers conducted on the sixth, revealed widespread rumors and misinformation among the students as to the state of the basketball team and also revealed student-faculty attitudes toward Jim Barns. Among the rumors uncovered about the Tigercats was the belief that the funds of the athletic department had been taken away by Barns and that the championship team would have to hitchhike and carry brown bag lunches in order to get to the road games on its schedule. The PTA charged that Mr. Lezacky, an assistant coach and an art teacher, had played a significant role in spreading these rumors among teachers and students. Student information also attested to a direct involvement by Lezacky in the anti-Barns protest of the previous afternoon: Lezacky had provided class time, school materials, and his own assistance in making the posters protesting Karniak's "removal" and denouncing Barns.

When asked about the rumor that the athletic department had been stripped of its funds, Karniak denied the report and stated that there had been more funds available for athletics under Barns than at any other time prior to Barns' appointment as principal. Investigating the athletic fund account, the PTA discovered that, during the period Jim had been principal, the athletic department had spent $15,000, leaving a balance of $5,000. More than $12,000 had been spent on the basketball team alone. This was hardly the accounting of an impoverished team or department.

The PTA also found that the majority of the students and teachers interviewed approved and supported their principal in his efforts to raise the educational standards and academic achievement of the students, to require all teachers to spend their time teaching, and to encourage all staff to stress the total welfare of all students.

Concluding their initial investigation, the PTA summed up its analysis of the problem in the words of one of its leaders. It was a situation in which Barns, wanting to okay expenditures from the athletic fund "didn't sit too well with the athletic department. It seems that the athletic department has been running itself as it sees fit." Meanwhile, on the same day as the PTA investigation—February 6—Barns made his first public statement to the press and defined the problem succinctly: "No school should run an athletic mill. It should be concerned with the education of students. Karniak's first job should be as a teacher of physical education; his position as coach is secondary." Rumors and conflicting reports continued to confuse the issue and the PTA, now quite concerned over the seriousness of the crisis, decided on emergency meetings, including one with Superintendent Fondy.

Before the PTA could carry out its decision to have an emergency meeting with the school administration, there was another student demonstration. But this time the protest, held by sixteen to twenty students in front of Barns' home on February 7, was against the principal's resignation. Student leaders, athletes, and ordinary students marched with signs reading "We want Barns" "If Barns goes, we go." Barns was not at home to see the turnout; he and his family were away in another city with the basketball team, but this symbol of grass-roots support was reaffirmed and amplified the next day when the PTA issued its first news release on the controversy. "The PTA appreciates the job he (Jim) has done in stressing education first and athletics second and in raising the moral and spiritual values through discipline and understanding the needs of our children." The release went on to announce a meeting between the PTA and Fondy to urge the superintendent to reconsider Barns' resignation.

In a letter to Fondy on that same day, the PTA made it quite clear that, despite hoopla hysteria and the obvious success of Karniak as a basketball coach, they would not be seduced by a winning team record into sacrificing good education for athletic trophies. The letter requested that Karniak be transferred, as it would be "in the best interests of the total school situation," and also asked for a transfer of Mr. Lezacky as a result of his suspected complicity in the student demonstrations against the principal and the feeling that he had used the students as "pawns" to further Karniak's cause. The PTA further requested the superintendent's approval of Barns' policies and expressed its regret that he had failed to receive the full cooperation of school personnel. Finally, the parent group requested that no action be taken on Barns' resignation "Until after additional information is secured through a public hearing at which all individuals shall be heard."

Karniak's gamble, in which he had put a twenty-year career and control of a winning basketball team on the line, had floundered. He had made his move at the peak of public basketball hysteria—and that hysteria peaks at no greater heights than in Iron County—when he was the coach of the number one team in the state. And he had anticipated and received support from his friends in the Diamond Club, many of whom were Central graduates who monopolized a section of seats under the basket at every game and intimidated referees. Diamond Club members had the political power of the machine and the ruthlessness to apply muscle against its opponents, and Jim was an opponent. Throughout the crisis, Jim's home was bombarded with obscene telephone calls, threats were made on his life, and rumors were rampant that certain political leaders were going to "get him" because Karniak was their friend. It was even rumored that these politicians owned businesses which benefited from contracts with the athletic department. Jim was not intimidated. He brought out that Smith and Wesson and stuffed it in his overcoat when he traveled alone. But he was rarely alone. Men, members of his staff and friends from C.A.B., escorted him to and from games and other school functions and set up a patrol around his home at night. When Jim drove to games—and he went to every one during the crisis—his car was proceeded and followed by cars driven by friends so he would not be "accidentally" run off the road—a favorite trick of the political thugs in Iron County.

What Karniak had not anticipated was that the conflict would throw the grass-roots community into gear and that they would stand behind the man who was helping their children to learn rather than behind the man who was winning basketball championships with their children. Supporting Barns, the community itself refused to be intimidated and continued to pressure the powers in the central administration and the school board for a just and educationally sound solution to the crisis.

On the day following the press statement by the PTA, Karniak did not show up at Central. His assistant coach, who was suffering from gout, was also absent and under a doctor's care, so Jim ordered a poll conducted among the teachers to select someone to train and supervise the basketball team because it appeared that Karniak might be out for an extended period of time. The majority of the teachers, given the option of voting or abstaining, decided the assistant basketball coach—the logical man whom Barns would have selected himself—should take over the team. The freshman coach was to supervise the team until the assistant coach returned.

The next day, February 10, one week after Karniak had released the news of his resignation to the press, a school board meeting was convened to consider the Central High School situation. The PTA presented its own petition and those of several community organizations within the Central High School area requesting that Barns be retained as principal. In his testimony to the board, Barns presented figures which showed that the major portion of the athletic funds went to basketball and football with the other seven sports receiving minor allocations. Karniak, who was still officially absent from Central, did attend the meeting, but made no refutation of Barns' testimony nor any statements elaborating his reasons for resignation. It was a heated meeting with many exchanges, but a statement from Barns keynoted the crisis. A heckler from the audience, one of the physical education teachers, had called out, "You two boys (Karniak and Barns) ought to sit down and work these petty disagreements out." Jim rose to his feet, the strain and harrassment of the past week etched in fatigue on his face, but there was no questioning his power, his dignity and his uncompromising refusal to brush this conflict and the future of Central high school with it, under the carpet. "There may be some boys in this room," came Jim's reply, "but I am not one of them, I am a man. These are not petty differences; the issues are fundamental." No action was taken by the Board of Education that day, and the crisis dragged on, awash in administrative irresoluteness.

The following day found Coach Karniak still absent from Central but with two announcements stating his position. One came from his physician and indicated that Karniak would be out for an indefinite period of time and the other, later in the day when the board still had not acted, came from Karniak himself, declaring that he would not return to Central High School until a decision had been reached on the whole issue. Meanwhile, the assistant basketball coach had returned to Central and was placed in charge of the Tigercats for the rest of the season. They were facing a tough contest on the following night against the runner-up Wildcats in their second to last game.

The twelfth of February turned into a crucial day for Central, its principal, and its PTA, as well as for its Tigercats. The basketball team, minus Karniak, kept up its winning pace, but barely, squeeking by the Wildcats in a 65-62 game. And, after a marathon private meeting the Stackton school board announced through the superintendent that Jim would be retained as principal and Karniak's request for a transfer would be honored. No decision had been made, as yet, on the PTA's request for the transfer of art teacher-coach Lezacky, but ultimately he would remain at the school. The final act in the drama came three days later. The Tigercats completed their undefeated season with an 88-59 victory over Clark, and the school board announced that Karniak had been transferred to a junior high school in an all-white area where he would serve as a physical education teacher. He would have no coaching duties.

Karniak had lost it all. Confronted by the unexpected and under-estimated power and tenacity of the Central High School community, the school board, and the politicians behind them had backed away from Karniak, fearing that to pursue the issue would eventually threaten their power base. At this time, two of the nine council members in Stackton were black, and both were supporting Jim Barns. With the black voting population approaching a majority, the local machine refused to turn the education issue into a full-scale political one. Nevertheless, their political base had been undermined with the encouragement to grass-roots power and black organization given by the community's successful fight. The same individuals and groups who led the grass-roots struggle against Karniak expanded their activities after the controversy and became involved in political problems and issues dealing with housing and police protection. Barns was not immediately involved in these activities—his time and effort were concentrated on Central High School reform—but his stand against Karniak had made him a prime target for pressure and harrassment from the political machine. Rumors continued to fly: Jim had "made waves" and his success in upgrading Central were a particular embarrassment to the superintendent's contrasting lack of action during his own previous tenure as principal at Central. In May of 1965, there were unconfirmed reports that a clandestine movement was under way to remove Jim as principal because he could not be controlled by central office. The PTA expanded its own activities and established a committee to monitor and act on all rumors. For whatever reason, the alleged conspiracy against Jim did not materialize and Jim remained at Central.

Central was not to be the same after the Karniak incident. The basketball team went into the state tournament where they played exceptionally well, advancing to the final game where they were defeated in overtime by two points. But, supported now by neighborhood groups in his programs to reform Central, Jim began to get the response from central office that had been promised to him before he accepted the position as principal. Painters and workmen descended upon the old building and began to make long overdue repairs, and the students, under the Neighborhood Youth Corps program, assumed the responsibility for maintaining the campus under the watchful eyes of full-time adult supervisors. The junkies, the winos, the pushers, and the loiterers were banished from Central's grounds and halls, and kept away by parents and students who policed the outside area. Attendance improved until it reached 88 percent, and Jim continued to press for academic achievement and improvements in the instructional program. He personally took charge of the efforts to get every athlete who could possibly qualify into some college. Honor students, average students, those who were interested and motivated, received special counseling and assistance. The push for college attendance was intensified. Counselors were required to see every graduating senior and to begin to identify juniors and sophomores with potential, and nothing was slipshod; records of every contact had to be kept.

In the early spring, a new basketball coach was appointed. He had served as a junior high school coach of basketball, baseball, and track for twelve years. He was the first black coach of a major sport in the history of the school.

The school year ended without major incident except for the graduation exercises. On that evening, when Jim rose to speak, the audience rose and he received thunderous and sustained applause from students and adults. It went on for five minutes. The superintendent of schools, Dr. Fondy, was recognized by polite applause.

For the next three years, Jim continued on his course. Teachers began to ask to be assigned to Central: both white and black teachers. The percentage of students graduating with honors steadily rose and the percentage going to college crept upward until it reached 30 percent of the graduating class. Within two years, almost every graduating senior varsity athlete went to college on scholarship or had the opportunity to go. One student who had the nickname "Happy" is a case in point. "Happy" was considered "slow," "retarded," "dumb." But he was a great basketball player. Jim got him into college where Happy not only completed four years of study but went on to star, in his senior year, as a member of the NCAA championship team. The list of universities attended by Central graduates grew to include Harvard and other Ivy League colleges as well as small white or predominantly white colleges in the West, Midwest, and East. Students also continued to attend black colleges in the South in ever-increasing numbers.

The mood was contagious. The boosters, athletic teams, choirs, band and orchestra lost their ragtag look. New uniforms were purchased as dances, dinners, raffles, and other fund-raising events were held with the proceeds going to the school. The overall climate of the school improved, but the educational program still left much to be desired. An improving school, even a good school, cannot eliminate poverty or drug addiction or alcoholism or despair. Nor can it replace ramshackle housing or stop juvenile and adult crime. What it could do was create a neutral zone within the school and its grounds, it could make the school an oasis of hope. These Jim and his staff were able to do.

In 1967 the decision was made to phase Central out as a high school and convert it to a junior high school. This was part of an overall plan to reduce the number of high schools and combine junior-senior high schools within the city. Eventually, three junior-senior high schools were to be eliminated. But, it was clear to everyone—Jim included—when this decision was made, that it was all over for Jim. Central was an old building located in the urban renewal area and it was a logical choice to be eliminated. It was also clear, however, that because of his activism and personality, Jim would never receive another high school principalship under the existing administration, It was also clear that he would not receive any other promotion.

Jim was neither surprised nor concerned over these developments. He had, in fact, been beseiged with offers from other systems, the federal government, colleges and universities, including his own alma mater. All offers had been rejected because Jim wanted to continue his work at Central; he felt he had a job to do.

The PTA greeted the situation with a mixture of anguish and hope. They knew a new high school building was needed for their children, but they also wanted Jim to become principal of the new high school. They were realistic enough to know that they could not have both. At that time, communities had little to say about the selection of principals, and, to complicate the matter, the new high school would be located in a completely different neighborhood. The superintendent would have to retain Jim as principal of Central, but there was no question that he would not move him to the new high school.

In 1968, Jim resigned and accepted a position with an agency in Washington, D.C., which had been created to oversee, coordinate, and direct multiple programs. This umbrella agency gave Jim an increase in salary and responsibility over that which he had as principal of Central. In his new job he continued to work with poor people and with the problems of housing, jobs, and mental health. Later he became director of a university program which trained city managers and public administrators, a position he now holds.

He had had a job to do at Central, and he had done it. He may not have done it all, but he did make a difference—a difference in pride, in power, and in potential for blacks at Central High School and for the people of Stackton. In 1967, one of the black council members who had supported Jim in the Karniak controversy, ran a victorious campaign for election as mayor of Stackton. A new era of black political power was symbolized in this victory, but the genesis of the struggle lay in the grass-roots battles such as the one fought by the Central High School community in 1965. These battles were commanded by a new type of leadership that Jim Barns embodied, a leadership that would not compromise rights or tolerate the forestalling of justice by accepting the patronizing advice of those who said, "Be patient."

Chapter Four

Laura

The office door burst open, and in rushed a small boy. "Hello, Reggie," said the lady pleasantly. "Have you come to see me?"

The youngster, still panting, held out his hand toward her. In it was a switch-blade knife.

"They, they want to take it away . . . but I won't let 'em, see!" he gasped, thrusting the hand and knife defiantly into his jeans pocket. The angry words lost their edge in the calm atmosphere of the room, crowded with desks, shelves, books, and cabinets. The youngster's hostility gradually subsided.

"Well, Reggie," said the lady, thoughtfully, as one sensible person to another, "you know it's against the rules to have a knife with you. Suppose you leave it with me for the day. I'll keep it safe, right here in my desk."

Her offer hung in the air as she gazed at him with an expectant smile. He fidgeted a little, obviously weighing the advantage of an honorable way out against the pleasure of maintaining his battle with the teacher upstairs.

"It will be quite safe here, you know," came the quiet voice, "and you can have it back later. But you must leave it at home after this."

A few more suspense-laden seconds passed. Then the youngster capitulated, a broad grin brightening the face so recently contorted with rage and fear. "O.K.," he said. Tossing the knife onto her desk, he dashed away as abruptly as he had come.

With a small sigh of relief, the lady put the knife into her drawer and smiled apologetically at the visitor. "I'm sorry for the interruption," she said. "Reggie is one of our youngest—and most troubled—students. He hasn't had much chance to discover that some grownups are fair and can be trusted."

Reggie is just one of hundreds of children who have begun to learn, perhaps for the first time in their lives, that one lady, Laura, cares about and respects them. She is a rare person. With seemingly endless patience, hardheaded realism and quiet determination, she is devoting her life to youngsters whose bitter experience of rejection has caused them in turn to reject themselves and their society. Nothing about her or her office indicates success or prominence, as men measure these things. She is slim and attractive, a quizzical twinkle sometimes enlivening a pleasant face that is too often lined with concern or fatigue. She is not the sort of person who stands out in a crowd or whose public addresses bring tears to the eyes of strong men. Nor is the Center, which she directs, imposing. Indeed, it is quite undistinguished, just one narrow brick house in a dispirited row on a block long since resigned to inevitable decay. Inside, the scars of decades of abuse and neglect have not been obliterated by enthusiastic applications of paint and bright carpet. Rats and roaches, one senses, have not been entirely defeated, but only temporarily evicted from a domain long claimed as their own.

In this decidedly unpromising setting without fuss or publicity, Laura is engaged in an infinitely worthwhile battle: to salvage the wrecks which a large city too often makes of the lives of its children. She began many years ago as a teacher in Maryland. She would have preferred to work in Metropolis, her native city, but openings were not available in its segregated schools. As a black teacher, she was eligible to teach only black youngsters in the few black schools. It was not until World War II, with its drain on existing manpower, that these rigid hiring policies were broken and she was able to return to her native city to teach as a long-term substitute. Several years later she was assigned full time to a special education school and began taking courses to obtain permanent certification as a special education teacher.

Laura admits that her chief motivation in agreeing to take on special education classes was the extra $300 pay, but she soon proved to be a teacher with unique concern for the youngsters in RE classes. Rebelling against the policies which reinforced their isolation from normal school activities, she instituted a number of hitherto unheard of programs: banking, field trips, group activities, and an honor system in the classroom. The youngsters' enthusiastic response spurred her on. Before long they were engaged in planning a senior trip to New York City to see the United Nations building. But innovation in the classroom was one thing; that could be overlooked by disapproving or doubting supervisors. A day-long trip out of town was something else! It took a special resolution by the city's Board of Education to authorize the trip, and the excited class had a wonderful time to cap their months of saving and making arrangements. It would have been much easier, in this and other situations, to accept the judgment of her superior; too complicated, too expensive, too dangerous, or whatever. But if Laura felt a project was *right,* she was persistent, infuriatingly so. She was willing to take her case right to the top, if necessary, and this time, at least, she had won. But this was only one of the many battles she would fight.

Another of her quiet battles was provoked by the grim and cheerless room in which she and her students worked. "The best remedy for dirty gray walls," thought the teacher, "is some fresh paint." But she had not reckoned with the bureaucratic response which is seldom direct and almost never practical. "Our schedule and budget do not permit repainting your room," intoned the people downtown, "and of course only our personnel and paint may be used."

Normally law-abiding and eager to please, Laura was enraged by this response. Quietly, she bought supplies, enlisted help and transformed the drab classroom into a cheerful setting for her program. Not surprisingly, the sky did not fall, no officials appeared to decry the unofficial paint, and the class settled down to see what this strange new teacher would do next.

Meantime Laura had learned something she had halfway suspected was true: it was much easier to avoid attention than to get it. If you need something from the system, prepare for a long hard campaign. But if you want to keep something from the bureaucracy—unless bombs or fireworks are involved—nothing could be easier.

Throughout her years of working with "disturbed" boys and girls, Laura continued to serve as their friend and advocate as well as their teacher. She visited homes regularly, and spent many hours trying to sort out youngsters with behavior problems from those who were actually retarded. Always her goal was to see that youngsters who were able could return to regular school at their own grade level.

Meantime her own growing family's needs forced her to seek a twelve-month position with a higher salary. She requested and was granted an assignment to the Youth Development Center, a residential detention home for juvenile offenders, all boys, whose offenses ranged from theft to assault and battery. Although administered by the state, the YDC educational program was run by the School District of Metropolis. Laura's friends and colleagues thought she was crazy. "Why go *there*?" they asked. "Don't you know those kids are absolute demons? Besides, they're all hopelessly stupid. You won't be able to teach. You'll be lucky to just keep from being attacked."

Undaunted by these predictions, Laura became the only woman staff member, took over a class, and started looking around to see what she'd got herself into. Discovery number one was that the YDC youngsters were neither demonic nor stupid. Indeed their biggest problems were these very labels, which had been placed on them by an uncaring school system and an insensitive community and which were likely to serve as a one-way ticket to lifelong trouble. Discovery number two was that YDC had not one high school level textbook for the entire crew of teenagers.

Horrified, Laura geared for action. Another shock came when she found out that neither the principal nor the special education division of the school system would provide funds to purchase essential books. Undaunted, she first spent her own money to establish a minimal collection of equipment, books (including some in Spanish for the Puerto Rican youths who had apparently been left entirely to their own devices by earlier teachers) and SRA reading labs. "It was awful," she recalls. "All the school had were namby-pamby Dick and Jane stories for kids who had been out on the streets, mixed up with hardened criminals and heaven knows what else."

She submitted a lengthy requisition—and the principal's response was "Where do you think I'm going to get this stuff?" Laura retorted, when she heard of it, "Either he's a fool or he thinks I'm one," and proceeded to telephone a nearby high school to beg for their discards. Her determination produced an avalanche of books—mostly trigonometry, Latin, and drama anthologies! But Laura persisted, backing up her requests for appropriate books with visits to other schools to find out exactly what was being used elsewhere. By the end of her first year, a reasonable collection of books had been accumulated, for the first time in YDC memory.

Painfully aware of her students' limited exposure to art and music, Laura also wracked her brain for ways to supply them with glimpses of beauty. The records, books, and pictures she brought in were a help, but they were not enough. The boys need to get away, she felt, to see and be part of the cultural life of the city. Metropolis' Art Museum may be its most imposing building, but it is its orchestra which stirs the pride of even unmusical citizens. It was not long before several YDC youngsters found themselves part of the Friday afternoon concert audience—an audience traditionally composed of white-haired befurred blue blood matrons. The boys' pride and enthusiasm (and decorum!) confounded the doubting souls who had envisioned riots within the staid Academy of Music.

Laura's earlier conviction that "special" youngsters needed to have the same kind of experience as their "normal" peers had only intensified during her years of successful experience. She began assembly programs at the Center, using movies from the public library, coaching students to put on their own plays, begging records and a record player when no pianists could be found to accompany singing. And she continued to take her boys on trips to Friendship Farm in rural Deer County as a favorite and frequent destination.

Laura might have stayed on as a classroom teacher, continuing to earn the affection of her students and the sometimes reluctant admiration of her colleagues. But when she became involved in advising and helping her students to arrange transfers to schools with stronger academic programs, she soon found that she was treading on sensitive toes. She was not a trained counselor and should not, said the "professionals," be exercising counselor's prerogatives. The fact that the YDC had no counseling had nothing to do with it, she would have to stop counseling.

But she was a realist; she knew she couldn't take on the whole certification system and win. Her argument—that successful experience should count for at least as much as formal classroom credits—had been made before and would be again. Someone else would have to stick with that battle. Meantime, she wanted to do whatever was necessary to see that her youngsters got a fair shake.

With the help of sympathetic allies, she obtained a fellowship for study at Columbia University and a leave of absence. A year later, armed with an M.A. in social-emotional disturbance *and* counseling, she returned to the YDC to become its first staff counselor. Now her main responsibility was to pave the way for YDC students who were ready to move back into regular schools. A major step for them was to attend school outside while continuing to live at the Center. But other schools were not as eager to accept her boys as she was to send them, and she frequently had difficulty convincing other counselors that disciplinary schools were *not* appropriate assignments for students who wanted to live down their delinquent past.

Another problem developed. Her superiors in the special education division were wedded to the notion of one-to-one counseling. Laura's own experience and training had convinced her that teenagers, and particularly YDC teenagers, were frequently uncommunicative or inarticulate in an individual office conference. But these youngsters could and did open up in a group setting. Wearily, Laura found that she once again had to connive and maneuver to do what she felt best for the youngsters. Group counseling took place at YDC.

Soon, however, she felt it was time to move to a position of greater influence, and she took and passed the exam for special education supervisor. Shortly after, she was assigned to one of the eight districts in Metropolis, and for the first time in many years, found herself without her own classroom or students.

Meantime, she had been giving much thought to a new kind of rehabilitation program for young people who had been in trouble. In her year at Columbia, she had learned that 75 percent of juveniles who served a sentence either returned to a penal institution because of new illegal activities or were killed or maimed by former gang associates who resented their attempts to change their behavior. What was needed, she felt, was a kind of "halfway house" whose chief purpose would be individualized assistance to youngsters for a period between detention and their return home. Laura had discussed her proposal with many people, including welfare authorities in Metropolis and in the state capital. But the responses were all the same: "A fine idea, but you're ahead of your time." Some people added the refrain to which she had long since grown accustomed: "Are you crazy?" "I'm really not," she thought to herself, but there were just so many bases to touch, and she had touched them all. That, finally, seemed to be that.

About this time, a new man came to Metropolis as the Superintendent of Schools, chosen by a dynamic new Board of Education. Everything in the school system was suddenly being studied, inspected, turned upside down and inside out. And special education was one of the departments into which the new administration's brooms swept first.

The board established a committee of experts to conduct a major collaborative study of existing and alternative ways to meet the needs of children with special problems. Knowing of Laura's interest, a principal in her district put her in touch with the director of this study. Just as she had decided to file her old proposal away permanently, she was asked to get it out, refine it, and join in the committee's efforts. It happened that one committee member was the director of a Quaker settlement house which had, among other things, been struggling to maintain an interim residential center for troubled boys. The program had been a complete failure, but the settlement still owned the site. Everyone knew the need still existed. Now in a promising turn of events, Laura had turned up with enthusiasm and ideas. Perhaps, at last, her dream could become a reality.

Until this point, Laura's battleground had been relatively limited. She had had plenty of experience in arguing with—or ignoring—administrative directives, in going after equipment, books or documents she needed, in confronting the "system" on behalf of her kids. But nothing had prepared her for sitting through endless committee deliberations, constant rewriting of her proposal, or negotiating with one official after another. In addition to the School District, the federal government, local agencies, and private firms (which wanted to get in on any potentially profitable contracts) were all involved. To someone used to daily immersion in the lively problems of real kids, the planning process seemed incredibly slow and ludicrously distant from the joys and agonies of youngsters in trouble. It was seldom clear where funds were to come from (or when), who made decisions (and when), or who would be responsible for getting any program off the ground (or when). Laura often went home on those days, wondering wearily whether anything could possibly come of all the talk and paper-shuffling.

But suddenly some things began to happen. Laura was asked to become coordinator for a new program to be launched at the Quaker-owned house. ("Had I been male as well as black," she notes wryly, "I would have been called the director, but Women's Lib wasn't around in those days to support my case!") The School District and the Quakers were each to provide enough money to get something started, but little else was clear to the newly assigned coordinator.

When she first went to look over her new quarters, Laura could hardly believe her own eyes. Dirty and dilapidated buildings were no novelty to her, but this—this was a wreck! Plumbing and heating had been dismantled; what little furniture remained was in pieces; rats and roaches were everywhere. And, most unbelievable of all, four boys—left over from the old program for whom the Welfare people had not yet found a new home—still lived on the premises.

Barely concealing her indignation, Laura talked to the director
of the old program, who did his best to dissuade her from thinking that she
might succeed where he had so patently failed. And when she stood firm, he
took his doubts away, to spread them wherever he could find an audience.

Anyone else would have fled in fury or dismay from this in-
auspicious start. Laura, however, had had her fill of meetings and proposal
writing. The house might be a shambles, but it was a real and concrete problem,
something she could tackle and vanquish. Maybe she *was* crazy, as her friends
had been suggesting all along, but she decided to stay. With the help of her
small inherited staff—a young secretary who doubled as a youth worker and
a couple of men—she set out to bring some minimal order out of the chaos.

Meanwhile, neighbors of the house, who were intrigued with the
sudden flurry of activity, were invited in to help plan the new program. Very
early it was decided that the official community advisory committee should
consist of men only. "So many black women had become active and well known,"
recalls Laura. "Some were connected with Model Cities programs, others were
trying to solve school problems. But the point is that there were just too many
of them, and a lot of men were getting really sensitive about their own role in
the black community."

For several months, Laura and her staff of three worked with the
committee to put the house in shape and run an informal nighttime counseling
and training program in such practical matters as filling out job applications. But
lacking funds and a specific mandate from either the School District or from the
local community, the halfway house idea stayed on the shelf.

Then the impact of public events once more reached into Laura's
life. A new crisis had emerged in the ongoing battle between the Board of
Education and city hall. The mayor was threatening to send police into the
schools to "solve" the growing disciplinary problems, and the board, opposed
to such extreme measures and yet dependent on the city council for approval
of its budget, was hard pressed to find an alternative. Someone brushed off
Laura's old paper, which presented a clear rationale for careful rehabilitative,
rather than harsh punitive measures to deal with troubled and troublesome
youngsters. The board used the proposal as part of its rebuttal to the mayor
and backed up its case by earmarking a large sum of money for new programs
for "disruptive" children.

Laura immediately swung into action and went down to put in her
bid for enough money to establish a full-fledged program and to carry it
through its first six months. Although her request was at first turned down,
she was determined not to let the matter drop. Instead, she called a friend in
the state capitol to seek advice—and found that he was not only willing but
in a good position to persuade a member of the Board of Education to get
Laura's funds. Meantime, a couple of highly-placed allies within the system had
been working to get her program off the ground. Within two weeks, Laura was

notified that funds were available. She had to discover for herself how to get staff on the payroll, order equipment, and get students assigned to the program. But somehow she penetrated the bureaucratic mysteries and found that youngsters simply gravitated to the house where, they had heard, something groovy was about to happen.

One of those kids who came was Nickie, a boy from a Kalmuk (Russian) family who had run away from his rigid home environment as well as the academic high school in which he had qualified despite his language problem. He had drifted around, working now and then to get enough money for the drugs which kept him from thinking about things too much. When he turned up on Laura's doorstep, he was on the verge of despair. Laura promptly arranged for treatment for his addiction, signing him in herself, and later permitted him to be the first of many "overnighters" who roomed with a staff counselor on the third floor. Having arranged for him to enroll in a new high school, she contacted his relatives and helped them to understand Nickie's difficulties, and found a Russian-speaking teacher who could talk and argue with Nickie in his native tongue. Not all her stories have happy endings, but in this case, Laura reports, the future is bright indeed: Nickie is an honor student, preparing for college and a career in physics.

Many of the students who had been referred to the Center were chronic truants, but in the spring of 1969, average attendance was almost 90 percent. Somehow, in an atmosphere which they described as "different" and "interesting," where adults "cared," they found it easier to examine their deficiencies and began working to remedy them. Perhaps even more important was the fact that the Center staff provided not merely educational assistance, they were equally concerned about the students' home situations, difficulties with gangs or problems with police and the courts. Teaching, counseling, appearing in court, visiting homes—all were in the day's work. Obviously, there was no regular schedule for anyone. The youthful staff members, like their director, were dogged in their determination to literally pull their charges back to a useful and satisfying existence. And, more important, they were armed not only with good intentions, but with training and experience in the arts of teaching, counseling, and social work.

As the school year was drawing to a close, and the money which Laura had managed to pry loose was almost gone, the staff went off for summer vacation, not knowing whether their jobs would be available in the fall. Fortunately for the students, however, a nearby black teacher's college had agreed to use some federal funds to bus students to the campus and provide a sports program.

Laura was again faced with serious financial problems. Day after day while the young people went happily off to take advantage of the campus facilities, she wrote and rewrote a proposal for continued funding. Her efforts at last seemed to satisfy school district officials and the proposal was placed on the agenda for the Board of Education's August meeting. The community, however, had some doubts about whether positive action would be taken. While an exhausted Laura flew to Puerto Rico for a much needed rest, the local community organized a delegation to attend the board meeting and ensure that "their" house would be funded. Whether their presence made a difference or not is a moot point. But Laura returned to learn that for the first time she had a reasonable budget for the year ahead and she would be able to concentrate on program development.

Quickly she gathered her old staff and added some new people. Unfortunately, there was little time to hash out philosophy and guidelines for the program—an omission which was to cost dearly in the months ahead. But students were already on the way, referred by principals and counselors in nearby high schools, and the immediate task was establishing rosters and assigning kids to specific tracks. They arrived in all shapes and sizes, their only common denominator being their inability to stay out of trouble.

It was soon apparent that the youngsters did not adapt to formal class schedules. The hastily established roster and track system had to be abandoned in favor of more flexible, individualized scheduling. Teachers were asked to conduct their programs in such a way that students could move from one room (and academic subject) to another according to their own interest and attention span. In the weekly group sessions, staff and students worked out agreements to ensure that each student spent some time each day in all the subject areas.

The strain of having to work out and adjust to new arrangements, while managing routine activities and frequent crisis, took its toll of the staff. They had not had time to talk through, let alone reach common understanding and commitment to the Center's philosophy. Day after day passed, each too full to allow lengthy staff discussion of what they were trying to do. Some staff members rebelled against any authority and structure in the Center. Others were too rigid to cope with a flexible student program. Meantime, distraught parents and frantic counselors in the schools were pressuring the Center to take just "one more" child who had exhausted all the alternatives. It was hard to say No, even though the facilities, supplies, and staff tempers were increasingly strained, almost to the breaking point.

By this time, Laura was losing even more sleep than usual in her growing concern for the Center's equilibrium. The youngsters *were* being helped—there was clear evidence of this in their growing sense of responsibility and in their academic gains. But all her efforts to smooth over, reconcile, and placate could not guarantee continued progress in the face of the staff friction. For a while, some help was in sight. A group process expert was enlisted to run a weekend staff retreat, during which goals, objectives, and strategies could be thoroughly examined. But the attempt to pull the Center together became a casualty of School District red tape: the necessary authorization could not be obtained in time, and the staff had to finish the school year without the badly needed conference.

By the time summer arrived, a more sensible or less commited person might well have been ready to admit defeat and throw in the towel. The constant pressure of administrative details, worry about funds, staff tension, problems of coordinating personnel from other agencies involved with Center students comprised a more than fulltime job. And Laura's life was complicated by the fact that the Center, although located geographically in one district, served four. Thus she was deprived of the benefits of a clear line of communication and counsel through a particular district office, in a time when the system was moving more and more fiscal and other responsibility to the eight district superintendents. Unlike an ordinary principal, or a person directing a program, Laura was pretty much on her own—a situation which was frequently a blessing, but could also be a distinct disadvantage.

Had Laura restricted her activities and concern to Center management, her working hours might have been reduced to something approaching normal. But in that small house, there was no protective distance, no inner sanctum to which she could retire to think and plan and write. In any case, she was constitutionally unable to move away from the teaching, counseling, and the nurturing role which she had played so successfully for so many years.

On many days, while reports or correspondence or official forms piled up on her desk, Laura could be found in the third floor lounge, or perhaps downtown on a shopping trip, dealing with students whose emotional problems were threatening to overwhelm them. A short expedition away from the Center was often the best method of preventing explosions or cooling down explosive tempers, and for Laura, the students welfare always came first. The routine business, more than not, had to be tackled late in the day or at home, when relative peace and quiet was once more available.

To those who knew her, and were aware that she had her own teenagers at home, as well as married children and grandchildren to fuss and worry over, she was a constant source of amazement and concern. Why would a woman who could easily have held a high salaried job with clearly defined responsibilities go on in such a grueling fashion? Advisors warned her that she couldn't tackle everything single-handed, that she might be *too* involved, that she would help no one by landing in the hospital. But the cost in personal terms seemed small to her when compared with the desperate need on the city streets and in the city schools. So she continued, sometimes enthusiastically, sometimes grimly, to see that youngsters who couldn't or wouldn't "fit" had somewhere to go and someone who cared about them. It finally cost Laura dearly. Laura was ordered into the hospital by her physician from pure, physical exhaustion.

But the rewards made that stay worthwhile. For example, one district superintendent, in addition to supporting Laura throughout the year, made a point to include in his annual report a statement praising Laura's Center as a "valuable and creative alternative to immediate placement of pupils in disciplinary schools." He further recommended that its services be widely expanded. But far more important to Laura were the changed lives of her youngsters.

Take Spider, for instance. Spider had served time in a correctional institution. Upon his release and return to junior high, his behavior was a constant problem. His attendance was irregular and when he did show at school, trouble inevitably ensued. A counselor phoned the Center in desperation; Spider turned up to look it over, and something clicked. For the rest of the school year, his attendance record at the Center was perfect and even though his academic progress was negligible, his relationship with and attitude towards the Center was good.

But over the summer away from the Center, with time hanging heavy on his hands, he got into trouble again. He and a friend broke into a factory, were arrested, and some months later, brought before a judge. The Center, to which Spider had returned in the fall, sent a staff member to court to plead his case, but the judge decided to commit Spider to another institution. He was, however, permitted to continue classes at the Center. The arrangement— and the solid support given him by the Center—paid off. Spider did very well academically and continued to prove himself responsible until he earned an early release. By this time, however, another summer with its attendant hazards had come around. What would happen to Spider?

Laura had been negotiating with the American Friends Service Committee to take some of her young people as members of its summer work camp program, and she recommended Spider for a position. Before long, the fellow who had seldom been outside the city limits found himself on a plane to New England, bound for a summer job as a swimming counselor in a camp for retarded children. Responsibility for younger and partly helpless children was the final ingredient in an alchemy which turned a hostile drifter into a more mature, self-assured young man. That kind of transformation justified, in Laura's eyes, all the frustrations and all the long hours.

Then there was Jimmy. He, too, was a chronic truant, whose every appearance at school resulted in an "incident" and a subsequent suspension. His mother who had six other children, had certainly tried to do her best. Jimmy attended weekly therapy sessions at a nearby clinic and received regular shots for his asthma. But now his mother was facing an operation and a lengthy convalescence. Jimmy was her biggest worry.

The Center magic worked again. The mixture of love and flexibility, combined with firmness and high standards—all too rare in Jimmy's school experience—encouraged a frightened, tense little boy to blossom into a self-reliant and confident fellow. Somewhere along the line, the allergy shots and therapy sessions were abandoned. They were no longer needed. Jimmy had friends and interests and a place where he was welcome.

Whether small successes like these accounted for Laura's devotion to a tiring and difficult job, probably even she couldn't say. But another summer found her once more looking toward a new school year. Fortunately, funds were assured long enough in advance so that she could line up a staff and get them together for two full weeks of evaluation and planning. Laura herself now knew better what kind of people made the Center work. They had to care desperately about kids, not be put off by hostility or insolence, and be willing to spend inordinate amounts of time to reach tough, frightened, angry youngsters. They had to be well-organized, yet not rigid. They had to be loving, yet not sentimental. Above all, they had to be "unflappable." Whatever the Center *was*, it was not predictable.

The third year looked more promising, not only because the staff was together, but also because a large array of supportive services had been enlisted: educational psychology graduate interns and undergraduate tutors from a local university; mental health consultants from a hospital; social welfare department aides. The school district, too, had assigned its research office to design and carry out a professional evaluation of Center progress.

Even so, problems continued. One young man, shortly after joining the Center, was arrested for a series of highly publicized rapes in a middle-class area of the city. The newspaper stories, referring to the Center as "his" school (despite the fact that he had been there only a few days), did nothing to improve the Center's image. And there were always critics lurking who firmly believed that the Center's approach was foolish: much better to penalize and incarcerate, they thought, than to understand and support youngsters who had gone wrong.

Then, too, the occasional drug addicts who came to the Center were the cause of grave concern and intense discussion among the staff. It was clear that these youngsters needed almost full-time, one-to-one supervision and help. The Center could ill afford to provide such intimate support without depriving other needy youngsters. On the other hand, these kids were at the Center because other solutions had failed and no alternatives could be found. How could they, who responded at least some of the time, be turned out on the street?

The small house, with all Laura's dedication and the ingenuity of its staff, was ridiculously insufficient to meet the demands placed upon it. It was already too crowded for all the activities the staff wanted to try—yet parents, counselors, and welfare or court workers kept calling the Center with monotonous frequenty: "Can you take Johnny?" "I have to find a place for Maria." "I'm at my wit's ends—if you don't help Sal, who will?"

That the Center was so small was sad enough, but the real tragedy was that it was unique. There should have been dozens of centers, all over the city, to provide troubled youngsters with the support and warmth and firmness which they needed so badly. But too many people did not even know the need existed, or, if they did, were too busy or too apathetic to care. Once in a while, when a crime was committed, a drug addict found dead in an alley, there would be a flurry of hand-wringing and pious editorials, until the crisis passed, drained of its catalytic possibilities by the flood of emotion.

Were there no other Lauras in the thousands of teachers who faced a classroom each year? What turned one woman's teaching career into a quiet, personal lifelong crusade to see that some problem youngsters got a fair shake? What gave this woman the determination to "fight city hall" and lose and come back to fight another day, and another and another?

Like so many unsung heroes and heroines, Laura is too busy doing her job to accept speaking dates, write articles, and earn herself a reputation. Indeed, she is almost unknown, even in her own school system. But Nickie and Spider and Jimmy remember her. Teachers, amused or amazed by her indefatigable efforts to make the system work for kids, remember her. Perhaps even those whom she could not reach retain a warm memory and a flicker of hope, because she cared and they knew it.

Laura continues in her program. The Center has survived and is working. To many Americans, size or speed in reaching a goal are the only criteria for success. Judged in terms of either, Laura's venture would be considered an abysmal failure. But today a visitor to the beat-up house on Franklin Street is struck by something—the atmosphere of happy confusion, an oasis of calm contrasting with noisy activity. The Center is not just a house, it's a home. A home where a group of young people whom life has cheated are learning to handle themselves and trust their fellow human beings. Perhaps that can happen only in small settings, like a family. Perhaps the process must always be slow. But a failure because it isn't big and fast? Spider and Nickie and Jimmy don't think so.

Chapter Five

Mr. T.

There were six students assembled on the stage of Roosevelt's auditorium. They were panel members selected to address the 1973 class of sophomores just entering Roosevelt; to give initial information about the high school and to answer any questions afterwards.

The faces of the panelists were expressive: eager and confident as they talked and gestured among themselves while the new students filed into the auditorium. The entering students had evidently heard a great deal about Roosevelt judging from the snatches of conversation floating past ones ears: "Yeh, my sister says they have this dance group that toured Europe." "The basketball team is out of sight." "My brother belongs to the jazz club." And now they were here—tenth graders—finally going to Roosevelt. (Roosevelt changed over from 9-12 to 10-12 in the late sixties.)

When everyone was seated and looking expectantly towards the stage for something to start, the six students glanced from one to another and back again to see who was going to speak first. Finally, and seemingly arbitrarily, a tall, handsome young man stood up and walked to the podium. The chatter of the auditorium began to quiet down. The young man just surveyed the audience for a couple of seconds saying nothing. Then with an almost innate sense of timing that would have impressed most professional speakers, the young man let the precious, quiet fill the auditorium. And in those last two seconds of silence before someone had to stir or cough, he leaned into the microphone—"Welcome to Roosevelt," he said in a whisper.

The applause was explosive and shouts of "Hey"-"Yeh now" could be heard all over the auditorium. The young man leaned back from the mike and smiled. The assembly was off and running.

This was a Roosevelt student—standing straight and self-assuredly quiet before an audience of applauding young people. His impressiveness was not lost on the entering students who were sitting up straighter in their seats in an almost unconscious imitation.

The young man give his name: Michael Hopkins, president of the senior class. He then went on to introduce the other panel members. Not all of them had titles, but each of them came to the podium to speak about Roosevelt.

There were many things discussed during the assembly: The sense of family felt at Roosevelt; the love, caring and concern shown by the faculty and administration; the encouragement and sustenance given to any troubles or triumphs; how the teaching staff has set a definite purpose—to prepare the entire student body for their future endeavors. But most importantly, along with the caring and concern demonstrated by the faculty, Roosevelt's faculty knew their stuff. And if one teacher was unable to come up with an answer to a question, it was either researched by the teacher himself or else the students were sent to the people or sources who did know. This is what Roosevelt was about in 1973.

After the panelists had each given their talk on Roosevelt, a question and answer period ensued. "What are exams like?" "Are there a lot of clubs?" "What are the requirements for student government?" "What kinds of scholarships are available?"

There were some questions, however, that weren't asked during the assembly. And these students no more needed to ask them than they would have questioned the chairs they were sitting on: "Why does Roosevelt have so many clubs and activities?" "Why is Roosevelt so beautiful?" "Why does Roosevelt produce so many college-bound students?" "Why do Roosevelt teachers and administrators care so much about students?"

There was probably only one person who could completely answer those kinds of questions had they been asked, but he was not present at this particular assembly at Roosevelt. He knew the answers simply because he had asked them at one time in their original form: "Why can't Roosevelt have a beautiful campus; Why can't Roosevelt students be proud of themselves and their accomplishments? Why can't Roosevelt faculty love and care about students?"

He had asked himself these questions long ago and had answered them himself. But in such a way that they would never need be asked again.

The time is 1970 and it was the end of an era. Three of the people sitting at the head table represented the past and the future. There was Mr. T., principal emeritus; Warren Wilson, retiring principal; and Robert Smith, principal elect. The first two men represented forty years of leadership in a school which was barely more than forty years old. In that period of time the school had produced almost 12,000 graduates; it had sent almost 3,000 to college and 1,100 had received degrees and entered the professions.

Four or five hundred people were packed in the banquet room. They had come from all over the country to pay tribute to Mr. Wilson, but they had also come to express their loyalty to the school and to the two men who had built it. When someone announced that over 40 percent of the current graduating class of 650 was entering college, the announcement was greeted with warm applause. This audience had come to expect such announcements. For many in the audience, it was hard to believe that it had not always been that way. And yet, this was a sophisticated and cosmopolitan audience in many ways. There were psychologists, laborers, physicians, housewives, lawyers and politicians, clerks and secretaries, and businessmen, electricians and photographers, old and young, men and women. The one thing they all had in common was an allegiance and loyalty to the school. Maybe it was pride. Whatever it was brought them back to the alumni reunions year after year.

What was it that brought people here to this school year after year? What was it that generated such long-term loyalty to a high school; clearly unusual, but easily understandable. It could be traced to an era that was ending. Two of the men sitting at the head table has been responsible for developing the esprit of and the institution called Roosevelt. One of them had been particularly influential. His name was Mr. T.

He was the boss. Make no mistake about that. Always correct; standard white shirt, two-piece dark business suit, subdued tie. Usually unsmiling and brisk, but courteous and not unfriendly. Everyone knew he was the boss: students, teachers, parents, the superintendent, the Board of Education. He never said he was the final authority, you didn't have to be reminded of it. But if you ever forgot, you wouldn't forget again. There was a pride and dignity about "Mr. T." He understood power and he had the inclination and the will to use it when necessary.

Looking back over the years one could relive a typical assembly program in the school. The halls are empty and quiet. Approximately 60 percent of the students are in their classes and instruction is proceeding as usual. But in a large auditorium filled with black students, teachers, and parents in an aura of rapt attention and excitement, all eyes are riveted on the man at the podium: his right fist raised and clenched; the forefinger extended toward the ceiling, his words flow with an eloquence and spellbinding power in a style reminiscent of the black gospel preachers or the stars of the Chautauqua circuit. The content is a tapestry woven from the vast storehouse of a well-educated man and inspired by an intense pride in the virtues, potential, and power of black people through the ages. As the speaker finishes, the audience responds in explosive support of the message and in adulation and respect for the man who has brought it to them, in his very being as well as in his words.

It is not the 1960s or the 1970s. It is long before the days of Black Power and Martin Luther King, Jr., and Malcolm X. It is Steeltown, U.S.A., in the midst of the Depression, and the auditorium is in a school that the official literature of the school district described as late as 1954 as a school built for the "little colored children."

And the man at the podium is Mr. T. This is his school; the people in the audience know him as principal of Roosevelt, but, to them, he is more than just a man filling an administrative position. He is their man; he is the boss; and for the next thirty years as principal of Roosevelt he will demonstrate and imbue the power of his belief in black pride by building his school and the surrounding black community into a very special thing. So special that alumni would return in staggering numbers year after year to express their loyalty to Roosevelt and its architect and to point with pride that their beginnings were here with Mr. T. And the school in turn would take pride in its alumni, a number of whom could be found in the vanguard of black achievement and reknown throughout the country.

As the audience moves out of the auditorium and back to classes through halls lined with the pictures of black men of achievement—George Washington Carver, Benjamin Banneker, W.E.B. DuBois, Toussant L'Overture, and Frederick Douglas—the air still rings with the echo of Mr. T.'s words and the strains of the assembled singing the Negro National Anthem, "Lift Every Voice and Sing," which opens every Roosevelt assembly. The faces in the halls reveal that the students are of all ages from the level of kindergarten through twelfth grade, for like other schools in Steeltown, Roosevelt is a unit school, part of the Wirt plan of organization popular during the thirties. These were difficult times when many children had to end their formal education before reaching high school, and the Wirt K-12 unit school gave every age level an opportunity to use the facilities and be exposed to all the dimensions of the work-study-play plan rather than delaying such experiences until the high school years. The unit school also provided an educational continuum and an opportunity for cooperation and apprenticeship between the younger and older students. And there are older students still, older than even high school senior age, some in fact the same age as that of the youngest teacher. Again, it is the irony of the depression which forces some out of school too early and gives others no place to be and no opportunities except school.

In a time when hope and dignity are difficult to come by, Roosevelt would become an oasis of promise and pride and a cornerstone for many individual's self-respect. This was Mr. T.'s one goal when he came to Roosevelt in the early thirties and one which stayed with him throughout those thirty years that he led the school.

The faces in these halls tell another story besides that of the depression; they tell part of the story of Steeltown, for all of the faces are black. Black children went to black schools; white children went to white schools. There were some exceptions, but, even in these, the separation of the races was underscored rather than diminished. The one exception on the high school level was the Frederick Leveret School, but the reason it was integrated was that Roosevelt was so crowded; it simply could not absorb all of the black students. And there were black children who lived within a block of Leveret some right across the street from the school. And there were white students who lived in the shadow of Roosevelt. But the white students who lived near Roosevelt always attended other schools, usually Leveret. The black students at Leveret attended the same classes as the whites and were allowed to participate in varsity football, basketball, and track. There the integration ended. Swimming pools were restricted to whites, as were the band, the orchestra, and the right to hold office or vote in student elections. Nor could the blacks attend the senior prom or May Ball—there were separate social affairs and student organizations for black students. And all of the teachers, coaches, counselors, secretaries, and administrators at Leveret were, until the 1950s, white.

Among the unit schools in the city, there was an Eastern High and a Western High, both of which occupied the same site, but Western High was for white students, Eastern High for blacks. Each race attended its separate school in different buildings, were taught by different teachers, and played on different athletic teams. All of the teachers in Western High were white, as was the principal. All of the teachers in Eastern high were black. Before he had come to Roosevelt, Mr. T. had been principal of Eastern High and for twenty years after his appointment to Roosevelt, Mr. T. would be the only black secondary principal in the city. It would be still another five years beyond that before another black high school principal was appointed.

It was, in fact, to facilitate this separatism on the administrative level that Mr. T. was made principal of Roosevelt in the first place. He did not come to Roosevelt as an answer to the school's quest for a man who could revolutionize the institution, body and soul, although Roosevelt did need such a man. He was, instead, selected by the all-white school board of Steeltown to serve as a buffer between them and "the coloreds." It was the practice of teachers in Steeltown to complain to the superintendent's office when they were unhappy with their principal. Black teachers were no exception. The essential difference was that the superintendent did not want black teachers constantly visiting the central office with complaints that should have been handled in the school. The school board and the superintendent wanted a man who could eliminate this problem.

When Roosevelt's former principal departed in the early thirties, the school board found his logical successor in Mr. T. He was, after all, the best trained black man in the Steeltown system, and, in fact, Mr. T.'s training, like everything else about the man, was rather special for those times. In the depression, when most teachers, both black and white, were graduates of two-year normal schools, and most principals, if they had earned degrees, had completed only the bachelor's degree, Mr. T. had an impressive and varied background of training and experience. It began with graduation from high school in his early teens and a degree with highest honors in mathematics and science from a small black college in his home state of Texas, followed by another bachelor's degree, this one in education, and experience in a Louisiana high school as both teacher and principal. And finally, there was the master's degree and advanced work from Teachers College, Columbia University, where Mr. T. supported himself and paid for his education by working at a myriad of odd jobs, including waiting tables and operating elevators. In Steeltown, he was also the only black man who had demonstrated his ability as a principal at a high school as a result of his time at Eastern. And he was, because of his education, personality and social contacts, the leading black in the city who was not a doctor or a lawyer.

And so, Mr. T. came to Roosevelt as principal. He knew when he took the position what the school board expected of him; he had been told as much, subtly but unmistakeably. It was one of the givens in the black-white situation into which he had come as an educator. For a man of his convictions, Mr. T.'s acceptance of such a role represented a compromise, but part of the fight and effectiveness of his leadership was the ability to reach for the ideal by understanding and working with the very real conditions which confronted him. It was so with Roosevelt, the school Mr. T. intended to make as good as, and hopefully better than, any other school in the city. What he admitted only to himself and a few intimates was that he intended to make Roosevelt the best public school in the country for poor black children.

With the power of a strong man and the skill and patience of a long distance runner, Mr. T. turned the school board's mandate into the foundation of his power and the beginning of Roosevelt's transformation. He began by insisting that the school board make him principal in fact as well as in name, and the school board responded willingly, for their buffer, to be effective, had to have power. This gave Mr. T. the opportunity to begin to develop the faculty as the backbone of the school's development and the creators of the school's new spirit.

Before the era of Mr. T., all faculty assignments had been made, as was the procedure with all schools, by the central office. With the coming of Mr. T., the procedure would technically remain the same, but, in fact, nobody was assigned arbitrarily by central office to teach at Roosevelt. Mr. T. always had the final word. This power was not his by delegation or procedure but a practice acquiesced to by the central office in the face of Mr. T.'s persuasive arguments on behalf of quality education for his students and his rigorous and dedicated search for faculty who would provide that quality. Mr. T. built his control by effectively absorbing a responsibility that others in the Steeltown administration were willing to abdicate to him. It was a propitious beginning.

The entire country was Mr. T.'s catchment area in his search for faculty. Friends, acquaintances, and colleagues in blue and white collars were contacted for nominations of promising black teachers. The black half of the dual school system in the southern states was raided, and the faculty began to grow in breadth, depth, and commitment. Mr. T. cajoled and bargained, searched and persuaded to get the kind of teachers he wanted. Each record was checked and double-checked, transcripts were scrutinized, hobbies and interests reviewed, commitments and educational beliefs assessed. Mr. T. interviewed and approved every teacher himself, and most who finally received appointments were recruited personally by him. His requirements were simple: dedication, academic achievement, and absolute loyalty to the school, the students, and the principal's goals. The people on Mr. T.'s staff had, above all else, to believe in those black students. If teachers demonstrated competence in teaching and spent their classroom hours teaching, they had nothing to fear from the principal. Even if he did not like an individual personally, the teaching performance was the crucial determinant of the relationship. If the children were learning, the teacher could do just about anything he chose: adapt or revise the curriculum and use whatever techniques seemed appropriate.

Mr. T. had wisely decided that the quality and dedication of the faculty was the single most important factor in his plan. And he was fearless and totally dedicated to attracting the best. His assistant principal was an English scholar with graduate degrees in English from the University of Michigan. His teachers had earned degrees from the top colleges and universities, black and white, in the country. Some of the colleges attended by Roosevelt faculty even in the early days were: Hunter College, University of Chicago, U. of Michigan, Indiana State University, Howard, Fisk, Hampton, Columbia, St. Louis, Washington, Ohio State, University of Kansas, Lincoln University of Missouri, New York University, Northwestern University, University of Illinois, and Indiana University. To assemble such a faculty during this period was infinitely difficult. During the 1930s and 1940s many white universities, including state colleges and universities, were far from hospitable to blacks even if they admitted them.

Mr. T. found and attracted outstanding teachers: Lila Lincoln, a lady known and loved by generations of students for her teaching of Shakespeare; Mrs. Lowell, head of the business education department, who placed girls in top positions in business all over the country; Charles Donnen, a "wild man," a scholar who made history and government come alive; Ida Long, senior sponsor and general impresario; Faith Denis, counselor, English teacher and a magician with children; Mr. Luckman, chemistry and physics teacher; Mrs. Mason, latin scholar; and on and on.

Mr. T. did not avoid controversy in his recruitment efforts. Two teachers recruited during the early 1940s illustrate his convictions. T. Richard Fulton and Edith Pernet were teachers in Virginia; one taught mathematics, the other English. Both epitomized the individualism, professional expertise, and dedication to students sought in his faculty.

You see, in the Virginia of the 30s and 40s Edith and T. Richard decided to confront one of the basic commandments of the southern dual system of education in which black kids went to black schools, white kids went to white schools, black teachers taught in black schools, and white teachers taught in white schools. And the black teachers were paid less than the white teachers regardless of their training and their experience. To put it mildly, Edith and T. Richard found this last point irrational and intolerable, and when they felt that way, they moved—people, organizations, institutions, and traditions. They moved this fight all the way to the courts, and won: black teachers and white teachers were paid the same salaries. And Edith and T. Richard were fired. They were fired despite the fact that they were outstanding teachers, kids learned from them, and they were leaders. Or, to say it another way, they were fired not in spite of these facts, but *because* of these facts. And so they came to Roosevelt, Mr. T. sent for them.

A short, stocky woman who stood four feet, eleven inches, Edith Pernet was an even match for the biggest and strongest student, parent or teacher that Roosevelt, or any other school for that matter, could boast. Bright and alive eyes that could fill with fire when she was challenged indicated to all that this was a fighter of a woman.

Edith was an English teacher at Roosevelt, and the juniors and seniors who were her charges found in Edith Pernet a task master—she had been a Master Sergeant in the WACs in World War II and knew how to command—whose discipline they respected because it was meted out with fairness, a deep concern for the student's welfare and sense of self-respect. She knew how to make students work without killing their adolescent spirit, and she was rewarded by the pride they took in the fruits of their efforts and the prizes they won in essay contests, poetry contests, and other literary competitions. It was some-thing to behold, seeing this four foot, eleven inch woman stand a six foot, six inch basketball player against the wall and tell him he was going to use his mind, write his papers, and behave like a gentlemen or she would personally beat him down to her size or break his arm. And then to see this big, adolescent kid grin with embarrassment and say, "Okay, Miss Pernet, you know I'm gonna do it for you." And if a student was a varsity athlete, she demanded that he main-tain at least average grades in all work if he wanted to participate in athletics. But she didn't rely on demands alone. She entered into secret agreements and operated in collusion with coaches, counselors, math teachers and others, not excluding parents, to enforce her demands. And she usually won.

That was the kind of teacher Mr. T. looked for, fought for, sup-ported, and took pride in, because Edith Pernet was the kind of teacher who knew how to do her job with her heart as well as her mind and whose first concern was the lives of her students. With that concern and that energy, it wasn't surprising to find her involved in a lot more than just teaching English at Roosevelt. She knew, as Mr. T. knew, that it isn't just disciplined learning that makes a school a place students attend, take pride in, and find identity. It takes more.

Inspired by her energy and organizational abilities, a booster club for athletic teams was organized at Roosevelt. So was a literary group. Miss Pernet transformed the senior year book from a drab document into a first-rate senior publication which won awards. The student government also progressed under Edith's watchful eye, as did a myriad of other activities. But for all their diversity, each activity in which Edith was involved spoke of her one abiding concern: the students. Nobody was neutral about Edith. They either hated her or they loved her, but all of them followed and worked with her because she produced results.

Mr. T. understood the value of teachers such as Edith Pernet and made good his commitment to that ideal by getting the wherewithal to hire them and expending energy to find them, wherever they might be and bring them to Roosevelt. And the Edith Pernets would come to Roosevelt in the thirties and forties, fifties and sixties, and seventies. And, where once they had to be sought out and recruited, soon they would be coming themselves, searching out Roosevelt and asking to become a part of it.

But even Mr. T. made mistakes and he had to live with them. Not every teacher selected lived up to expectations. And when that occurred, Mr. T. took decisive action. Mr. Johnson was a case in point. A well-educated teacher of mathematics, Mr. Johnson was assigned to teach several classes of college preparatory students. They were the honor students with high test scores and good motivation who were doing well in all of their other classes with competent, demanding teachers. But, in Mr. Johnson's classes they were receiving D's. In one class of thirty-three students, twenty-one received failing grades and five, D's. In an Algebra II class, the record was even more appalling: fifteen out of twenty-one failed and one student received a D. In all other classes including chemistry, physics and English, the lowest grade received by Mr. Johnson's students was C. Moreover they were scoring in the top 20 percent on National Achievement tests and had superior scores on college board exams. Many became national achievement scholars. According to Mr. Johnson, the fault lay with the students. They were, he said, stupid, ill-prepared, and lazy and they were below average, not up to caliber of good white students in college preparatory classes in other schools.

Parents were angry, students were in tears, and other math teachers who had taught and tutored these students were at a loss to account for the behavior of Mr. Johnson. They were unable to persuade him to change his attitude, which at best was unrealistic and oppressive.

Mr. T. took over. He consulted with Mr. Johnson several times during the course of the semester, but the math teacher refused to change his stand and continued to insist that his Algebra I and II students perform at a completely unrealistic level to qualify for grades of A or B.

Now Mr. T., a former demanding mathematics and science teacher himself, saw clearly that it was not an insistence upon standards which was prompting the difficulty. It was a combination of things: Mr. Johnson's glorified notion of his own knowledge, an unrealistic image of how white students performed even though he had never taught white students, and a basic contempt for the abilities of poor black students. But more important than all of these, Mr. T. saw the ultimate result of such experiences on students: the crushing of their spirit and determination. This, of course, could and would not be tolerated. After repeated attempts on the part of the department chairman, vice principals and Mr. T. himself, there was no change. Accordingly, the following letter was sent to Mr. Johnson.

February 12, 1958

Mr. William Johnson
Teacher of Mathematics
Roosevelt High School
Steeltown

Dear Mr. Johnson:

Effective Monday, February 12, we are transferring the pupils in your algebra classes occurring at 8:15 and 11:15 to Mr. Robert Wells for the remainder of the semester. You will take the assignment which is now carried by Mr. Wells at those two hours.

This change is made because, apparently, judging by the marks which they receive, the pupils in these classes are not succeeding under your instruction. Many of these pupils' past achievement scores and present ability scores indicate that they can do the work normally required for beginning algebra pupils. It appears that there is a radical maladjustment either in the learning or the teaching situation.

A study of the distribution of marks given by you as appears in our summaries shows that approximately 80% of your pupils are not doing satisfactory work according to your evaluation, receiving either D's or F's. Less than 20% received satisfactory marks.

We have discussed this matter with you on many occasions and have discussed it in the faculty meetings on several occasions also, but the problem seems still to exist in your case. After careful consideration, we feel that it is best to transfer the pupils to another teacher in the hope that a better adjustment will be made. We shall arrange for a conference with you the first of next week concerning this entire matter. In the meantime, the Assistant Principal will discuss any details inherent in this connection.

Upon receipt of this letter, the math teacher went into a state of shock from which he did not recover for weeks. None of the students or faculty said a word to him about the reassignment. Nobody gloated, but Mr. Johnson had discovered once and for all what it meant to cross Mr. T., when crossing him meant the violation of the rights and interests of the students at Roosevelt. And, Mr. Johnson learned something about himself and something about teaching as well. When the lessons were absorbed, he became a better teacher for his experience with Mr. T.

ADMINISTRATIVE ORGANIZATION

Mr. T. knew he needed help from his assistant principals. He also knew that opportunities for advancement were limited for black administrators. He therefore organized the school into two schools. Mr. Wilson became principal of the elementary school and assistant principal of the high school. Later, when Mr. T. had several assistant principals, he assigned one as principal of the elementary school, one as principal of the junior high school and both were assistant principals of the high school. Mr. T. in effect was supervising principal of three schools. In so organizing his operation, all of his aides gained experience in all phases of administration and supervision, an experience they would not have been able to get anywhere else within the school system.

OTHER PRIORITIES

Once you had a good faculty, you could begin to concentrate on other things. Unfortunately, Mr. T. couldn't concentrate all of his time in getting good faculty; other developments had to go forward simultaneously. Pride and discipline were especially important. Teaching was what it was all about, but you couldn't teach unless there was discipline. Mr. T. believed that a teacher, no matter how bright or well-prepared, couldn't teach anything if the class was raising hell. A teacher whose class was out of control had to answer to Mr. T. But, as most educators know, and as Mr. T. believed, discipline was not so much a question of control as it was one of cooperation, respect, pride, and a sense of doing something worthwhile. To get discipline, Roosevelt had to do its job as a school and that meant aim for excellence in academics and in the arts and to provide an aura of school pride and esprit de corps, to which athletics was obviously the key. But Mr. T. wanted academic excellence, excellence in the arts *and* athletic achievement. How to do it? Move forward on many fronts simultaneously.

As Mr. T. surveyed his school in the thirties, he knew that his struggle was on many fronts, and that faculty alone couldn't bring his dream into reality. When the school board appointed Mr. T. as principal, they brought under his domain a building, a corps of teachers, and a multitude of students, not a school in the way that Mr. T. defined school in his own mind. A school had to generate pride; it had to be a place where students, teachers, and administrators alike respected one another and the work they were doing together.

And, ultimately related to that pride and esprit de corps, generating from it and, in turn, supporting it, would be the standards of excellence, the discipline, individual freedom, and the development of more and more avenues of opportunity and enrichment. These are the goals that education sets today and struggles, often unsuccessfully, to achieve. The difference for Mr. T. was that these goals had to be achieved by black people for a black school, and the foundations had to be laid in the midst of the depression in a dual, racist system. The difference was Mr. T.

The question was, where to begin, and the answer was in the intertwinings of all aspects of school life: Mr. T. and Roosevelt had to move forward on all fronts at once, with greatest concentration on the critical problems and building on their solutions.

First of all, there were the physical aspects of the school itself. A school which generated pride had to be a school that looked like people cared about it. Mr. T. saw to it that Roosevelt was such a school. In so doing, he also found work and some much needed extra dollars of income for students who otherwise would not have had the few cents to buy the milk and hot meal that the school lunch program offered. Mr. T. put the students to work in the cafeteria, on the custodial staff, in the offices. Walls needed cleaning, halls and floors has to be sanded and waxed, walks cleaned or snow swept, uniforms, such as they were, had to be laundered, books and supplies had to be stamped and delivered. There was work to be done and the students had their part to play and they could be paid for their work too. NYA, PWA, WPA—whatever the alphabet soup delivered, students at Roosevelt got their serving.

Roosevelt had a large, beautiful front lawn with trees and shrubbery which was maintained by the custodial staff as if it were a piece of sculpture. It looked like a college campus. And woe be unto anyone, adult or student, who dared to set foot on that lawn. The school site itself was actually a collection of buildings: one three-story main building, two smaller buildings of brick construction, housing most of the primary grades and two wooden barracks-type portable buildings, housing the shops, the gyms, and the band room. And there was no graffiti to be found, inside or outside the buildings, in classrooms, in toilets, or in halls. The school was spotless. Behind the school, the playground was sand, the track was cinders donated by the local major industry, and the football field could charitably be called a mixture of clay, dust, and straw. Not everything was the way Mr. T. would have liked it to be. Roosevelt was a black school, and the black school received many of its supplies in hand-me-down fashion from the white schools. There was some new furniture and some new books at Roosevelt, but much of the furniture came from the white schools when it had been replaced by new furniture there and many of the books, especially those issued to the high school students, had already been used for several years by white students at other schools. Mr. T. hated it and fought against it, but there was only so much he could do about such matters.

As Roosevelt began to progress, Mr. T. used his community contacts and the weight of the parents' group which he had formed to get some of the equipment that the school needed. In the early days, Mr. T. led and dominated the parents' group, and the community learned to throw its support behind Mr. T. and force the school board to give Roosevelt things it should have received routinely, but, in fact, would never get without a struggle. It was a venture well-founded and nourished: when Mr. T left Roosevelt, the paid membership of the Parent-Teacher Association totaled more than 900.

Slowly the struggles began to pay off. Mr. T. demanded and received new pianos, many new band and orchestra instruments, and his kitchen equipment was first rate and new. Roosevelt had the largest auditorium in the school system, seating 1,300, and the equipment, draperies, and stage were first rate as well. When official channels dwindled or balked, the community took over with increasing enthusiasm and support. Fish fries and chicken dinners, outright donations and fund-raising projects of all sorts helped to get the necessary items. Sometimes they were castoffs, but what was lacking in newness and quality was more than offset in pride and enthusiasm.

In a short time Roosevelt would earn the reputation as the cleanest and best maintained school in the city. Mr. T. would sometimes chuckle over the fact that visitors, especially white visitors, were always shocked to see how well kept was this black school. Roosevelt would soon become the showcase for the black community and the center of what was happening for blacks in that city. There was no where else in Steeltown for certain things to happen except Roosevelt. Not in the midst of the depression in Steeltown to which blacks had come from the rural South, from places like Alabama, Arkansas, Mississippi, and Georgia, to find themselves settling with but separated from the immigrants from Poland, Hungary, Italy, and other parts of Eastern Europe. This was Steeltown, an overwhelmingly blue-collar settlement of first and second generation new arrivals, most, both black and white, with rural backgrounds. The middle-class mill people—the managers and superintendents—lived in Chicago or a small, separate compound near Steeltown, so there was no really well-defined middle class in the city.

Leadership in the black community was even more scarce. There were a few black doctors, lawyers, social workers, and ministers, one or two policemen, a few firemen—all assigned to one station—and a few mom and pop storeowners, and the black underworld. Everybody else worked in one of the industrial plants, except, of course, the teachers, most of whom were at Roosevelt, and Mr. T. and his administration. It was from here that leadership in the black community would come, if it was to come at all. There was no indication from central office, or, for that matter, from the community itself, that Roosevelt was expected to play such a role. Nor was there any support from central office until 1955, and, Mr. T. would be the lone black principal until the 1950s. The community responded as Roosevelt began to demonstrate its direction under Mr. T., and this reaction was hardly incidental or accidental. Mr. T.'s reforms showed the community that Roosevelt was a black organization that had the power to speak for and work for the interests of its people, and he was very careful to make these reforms visible and symbolic for the community as well as substantial for the students.

This aspect of visibility was one of the reasons, along with holding it as a basic pedagogical belief, that Mr. T. was especially concerned with the discipline at Roosevelt in the early years. Thus while trying to move Roosevelt forward on both the academic and the athletic fronts simultaneously, Mr. T. fortunately found that in each of these areas, Steeltown provided some special elements which could be used to Roosevelt's advantage if handled skillfully. One of those elements was the Wirt work-study-play plan popular in Steeltown schools in this era, and the other was a unique emphasis upon and an interest in high school athletics.

The Wirt plan, which had its beginnings in Steeltown in the first decade of the century, was a total schooling plan in which vocational and cultural activities would be as equal and integral a part of the curriculum as the academic studies. The practical and the theoretical, the learning and the doing, would go hand in hand in all endeavors. Such a plan provided great opportunities for innovation and expansion of school activities and promoted demonstration and sharing of these activities through the emphasis on the auditorium program. At least once a day various groups or classes in the school would demonstrate ongoing projects, hear speakers from the community or perhaps participate in music or art presentations. Eventually the plan would call for separate auditorium teachers whose exclusive job it was to plan, coordinate, and oversee the assembly presentations, speech, drama, and music classes. This was the nature of the plan that the Steeltown system was committed to, but the commitment hardly meant that the plan was realized in its full potential in the white schools, much less in Roosevelt where, before Mr. T., there was a constant struggle just to maintain a very basic academic curriculum.

So, when Mr. T. went after cultural and academic innovations at Roosevelt, he was hardly breaking precedent or making outrageous demands on behalf of his students. What he *was* doing, however, was to have the audacity to push relentlessly for innovations and additions that would keep Roosevelt at least on the level with the two schools that were considered academic schools in the city. He was never able to get the equivalent materials or space or support that those two schools received, but he managed to get enough to enable his students to gain access to colleges and universities and pride in the school's capabilities. Thus, over the years, Mr. T. changed the bare bones college curriculum—which had offered two years of math, two years of two modern languages, Latin and chemistry every year, and physics only on alternate years—to a broader curriculum which included five years of math, four years of two languages and two years of two others; physics, chemistry and advanced science every year.

Mr. T. provided for a number of cultural courses including music theory and composition, specialty singing, madrigals, and art.

In addition to a broad curriculum, the list of activities grew: marching, concert and dance bands, concert orchestra, madrigal singers, chamber music groups, brass choirs, boys and girls glee clubs, mixed chorus, cheerleaders, Hi-Y, student government, honor society, tutoring club, Masque and Gavel, ROTC, And the clubs seem to keep pace with the activities: chemistry, physics, art, math, Latin, French, Spanish, business, writers, social science, Orchesis, and nine sports, each with its group of student and adult boosters. Every student was scheduled for speech and drama classes at the elementary and secondary levels, and every student had to learn the rudiments of parliamentary procedure as part of his speech courses. "Classical" music was required study, but so was music by black composers including Negro spirituals and jazz. Art was required of all students, and it was taught in art classes by trained teachers of art. And, in every undertaking, quality achievements were sought and standards of excellence set. There was no reason, simply because Roosevelt was treated as a second class school in the system that its students or administrators or faculty should believe or act as if that were true. Thus, Roosevelt students entered into all manner of competitions—music, marching and dancing contests, oratory, debate, art—and, as the community watched and supported, the Roosevelt students started pulling in first prizes.

Roosevelt also competed athletically—not with the white schools, because that was forbidden until 1942—but with black schools wherever they could be found in Indiana, Arkansas, Texas, North Carolina, Virginia, and Missouri. When Mr. T. was seeing to the poetry and debating clubs and music and art, he was also seeing to it that Roosevelt had a football, track, baseball, basketball, and swimming team. It was particularly in and through athletics that Mr. T. saw a vehicle for developing discipline and pride, which in Mr. T.'s terms meant self-discipline and pride; and for a setting of standards of behavior that would apply throughout the school's activities. Athletics became the keypoint for two reasons: because the teams and their supporters had to travel to other cities and states to meet their opponents, Roosevelt would be on public display in these instances more so than anywhere else. And, in a rough steel town where students could sometimes be as old as the teachers and considerably bigger, it was the coaching staffs which contained most of the few men who were on the faculty in the early years and it was the coaches who assumed the job of being general disciplinarians.

At first the coaches had a rough time of it. They were all locals, reared in the city, graduates of local high schools, and outstanding high school and college athletes in their own right. None of this mattered that much to the students at first. Tires on cars were slashed; windows were broken, threats were made constantly—some in anonymous letters, some in veiled but menacing statements—and on more than a few occasions physical confrontations took place.

But the coaches and the physical education teachers stood their ground, and, as long as their actions were in the best interests of the students, they knew they could count on the full support of Mr. T. He stood shoulder to shoulder with his teachers, against angry parents, rowdy students, and central office. And when a student didn't toe the line, he had the unforgettable experience of a confrontation with Mr. T. Mr. T. could handle the biggest and toughest of his students. Yet, Mr. T. rarely used corporal punishment. His very being conveyed unquestionable authority and his verbal confrontations with a student, or with faculty if the conditions warranted it, were direct, emphatic, and disarming. His disciplining was never capricious or emotional or irrational. When Mr. T. had you on the carpet, you were told exactly what actions had brought you there, exactly what principles you had violated, and you had to face your failing and their consequences. Six foot, 200 pound young men, tough as nails, would swagger into Mr. T.'s office for one of those confrontations and emerge much changed, some not without the memory of their own tears and most with the realization that they had some shaping up to do and knowing exactly where and why.

In those rough days of the depression when going to college, or, for that matter, finishing high school was not a routine expectation for young people, Mr. T. and the coaches and the rest of the faculty made those students get down to the business of learning and exploring and believing in their own potential. But good behavior wasn't all the result of disciplining; most of it, as is always the case in good schools, sprang from the enthusiasm and respect the students had for Roosevelt and its activities. Nowhere was this more apparent than in the support and the esprit generated by the athletic teams. Roosevelt was building outstanding athletic teams in football, track, wrestling, swimming, golf, cross-country, baseball, and tennis.

In those early days, every resource was tapped and everyone was eager to help. The faculty pooled their own meager resources and bought a bus. It wasn't really a bus; it was a converted Ford welded together in sections and looking very much like the airport limousines of today. But it was enough to transport the teams to their games in small "colored" community centers or wherever they could get space to play. Food, gasoline, lodging, uniforms, and other amenities were paid for from the meager receipts from the athletic contests or from the pockets of interested faculty, parents, or community organizations. Athletes had to depend on hospitable blacks for their lodgings in communities where they played their road games as there were no public accommodation laws then nor any pressures for breaking down those barriers.

In later years, especially after Edith Pernet arrived at Roosevelt and with her, the newly organized booster clubs, the Ford bus, which had announced the presence of Roosevelt teams, would be replaced by a legion of buses filled with Roosevelt supporters. In Steeltown, U.S.A., high school athletics are unlike high school athletics any other place in the country—especially when it comes to basketball. Then that unique phenomenon known as "hoopla hysteria" takes possession of students and adults alike, game tickets became the most sought after commodity in the state, and the players and standings of the high school teams are known, analyzed, agonized and rejoiced over. By the 1940s, when the Roosevelt team traveled to distant points inside and outside the state, the boosters went with them. Not 100 boosters, or 200 or 500 or 600, but 700, 800, and a thousand—all on school buses supervised by teachers, all dressed alike in school sweaters, and all having a ball: singing, talking, cheering, joking, and jiving. This was Roosevelt on display, and, from the very first, the pride and deportment of the boosters was as much a credit to Roosevelt as were the successes of its athletic teams. Not once in the more than ten years that Edith Pernet was in charge of the boosters did the school ever receive anything other than the most complimentary phone calls, letters, and messages from mayors, police chiefs, teachers, citizens and black communities alike. They simply couldn't believe it. After all, the students were black. There they were, 700 to a thousand strong, acting in unison, enjoying themselves, and demonstrating pride in their teams, in themselves, and in their school.

Edith and Mr. T. and others involved would see to it that every student who wanted to go, could. Bus companies competed for the business from Roosevelt, and Edith drove a hard bargain, constantly keeping down the price so that even the poorest kid could attend. For active supporters who couldn't quite get the total price, there was a fund to underwrite their attendance. Free tickets were always available for deserving, indigent students. At one point, this activity found Edith embroiled in a major battle. The bus company that got Roosevelt's charter contract was not the local, privately-owned company. There was a simple reason for this: their price was too high and renting these buses would have forced Roosevelt students to pay a higher fare. So, Edith rented from a neighboring city and the local company responded with pressure, political influence, and finally, the threat of a legal suit claiming the other company was using unsafe equipment and unqualified drivers, some of whom were women. Edith wouldn't budge, and Mr. T. backed her. Finally, the local transit company lowered its prices and became competitive, and Edith began to use their buses also.

Through it all, the tough times and the good ones, coaches, teachers, vice principals, and principal counseled their charges, listened to them, argued with them soothed their damaged egos and wounded pride, applauded their triumphs, and spurred them on to the next hurdle. Tough stuff to pull off, but it worked. Being at Roosevelt began to mean something. For example, starting in 1962, when all the other recreational facilities closed down at 8:00 or 9:00 because of a lack of supervision, it was routine practice to leave the lights on until midnight outside on the back courts of Roosevelt high school so the students and neighborhood residents could play basketball and touch football Roosevelt students and community respected the building: no break-ins, no vandalism, the neighborhood really related to the school, cared about it and protected it.

The dropout rate was checked, and, one by one, at first, Roosevelt graduates took their places on college campuses. In the first graduating class of about thirty, six had gone on to college. In the thirties, Roosevelt sent students to the University of Chicago, the Big Ten universities, as well as to Hampton, North Carolina A&I, Howard, and Fisk. As the years passed, Roosevelt graduates found their way to Dartmouth, Grinell, Iowa, Illinois, Indiana, Harvard, Yale, Ohio State, Columbia, UCLA, Bowdoin, McMurray, Boston University, Wisconsin, Montana, Western Michigan, Kenyon, as well as Morgan State, Florida A&M, Morehouse, Atlanta, Morris Brown and Clark, more than 100 all told. Roosevelt didn't just send its graduates off to college; it was one of the wedges that opened colleges to blacks and it kept close contact and counsel with its graduates to assist them in their college experience. Revenues from school shows and athletics in the later years went into a fund for graduating students to help pay for their transportation to and from college interviews. And, it became the general practice that all members of the nine varsity teams would go on to college. Mr. T. felt that if he could get as many students as possible to college, even if they only stayed for one year, the experience would change their lives. And that was what the struggle was all about.

Not only college-bound students were helped. Relationships were established with local businesses, the major industries, and city government. Roosevelt graduates were fed directly into jobs and training. As the years passed, the school system hired many as secretaries, custodians, engineers, teachers, and principals. The task was to assist every graduate. Roosevelt was a community school as well. By the late 1950s a full-time evening school for dropouts and adults would be operating within the school building. An evening recreation program was also started.

By the 1940s, an increasing number of black students were attending another high school in the city. Neighborhoods and the times had changed and because some of the students lived across the street or within a few blocks of the other high school, they had to be admitted. Besides, Roosevelt was ridiculously overcrowded. The size of the graduating class had more than doubled. The black students at the other high school looked with awe on Roosevelt. They envied its image and its achievements and even respected its arrogance. Black parents connived, schemed, and lied to get their children into Roosevelt. It had become something special. Even the dropouts claimed Roosevelt! Despite discrimination, despite prejudice and racism and second class citizenship, Roosevelt had won some major battles.

Mr. T.'s dream for Roosevelt was becoming a reality, but, like all endeavors, it had its failures as well. The education wasn't always as good as it should have been. Many students didn't read at "grade level," but most of them could read. Everybody didn't graduate, and not all who could have gone on to higher education decided to or were able to do so. Sometimes the shrinking violet or the slow starter wasted a few years or got lost in the shuffle. Like any other school, there were shortcomings in this respect. But the school had become a source of pride, to the students and faculty and to the black community of Steeltown. Mr. T. had made certain of that. The things he did for Roosevelt were good in and of themselves—the athletic teams, the contest victories, the cafeteria run by the community and the students, the assemblies that brought in noted black speakers from all over the country—but they were also gestures of power and pride that the community could identify with and sought to be a part of.

In the days before Black Power, Mr. T. was its apostle and Roosevelt was its temple. The walls in the principal's office and the walls in the halls were lined with black men and women of achievement. In the days before the anguished cries of "Who am I?" Mr. T. told them who they were, and, even more, led them to a sense of black awareness.

In the middle of the civil rights movement of the 1960s, a life membership for Roosevelt students in the NAACP was paid for by students, faculty, and alumni contributions. Student civil rights leaders at Indiana University, Southern University, and Harvard came from Roosevelt. This type of action signified Roosevelt's commitment to black awareness. No one demanded that this be done—it was just the thing to do. In one year the alumni gave to Roosevelt two $1,000 academic scholarships. The alumni also bought Roosevelt three sets of uniforms for the school cheerleaders and sponsored the senior class picnic by picking up the costs of food and transportation—totalling almost $800.

Almost every black person of national achievement visited the school, spoke to students, and talked with faculty. In the days before the raised clenched fist, Mr. T., his right fist raised and clenched, except for the extended forefinger, saluted black men and women and his example and his oratory brought the students, faculty, and parents to their feet in response to his example. Black Power! For real!

The costs were high, especially to Mr. T. Three times in his career there was an acting superintendent appointed, and each time Mr. T. was over-looked despite the fact that his colleagues considered him the logical choice. The board was not ready for a black man. Time and time again Mr. T. would see needed additions to his physical plant postponed while schools in white neighbor-hoods received physical improvements, even though they were not nearly as overcrowded as Roosevelt. Once he had to personally contact his congressman and go to Washington to insure that a needed addition to Roosevelt would be provided through WPA funds. He got his addition, but even with such persever-ance, Mr. T. was sometimes criticized by his own people who thought he had not fought hard enough for the things the board failed to provide. Through the years he watched while outstanding achievements by Roosevelt students and faculty received only perfunctory citywide recognition while lesser achievements in other schools received full recognition. It was not an easy thirty years.

At first the percentage of students going to college were low. Slowly, the percentage of the graduating class going on to higher education went from 10 to 20 to 30 to 45 percent. The size of the graduating classes increased from 55 to 750 over the thirty years. And the scholarships kept pace with the number and percentages. Scholarships were usually sought according to the talents of the students: art, music (vocal and instrumental), athletics (girls and boys), academic, nursing, leadership ability. Each counselor tried to match college to student; teachers used personal contacts with friends and their own colleges. Roosevelt tried to place one or two students in a college and let them establish a track record, thereby making it easier to send several students to the school every year, thus building up a pool of colleges where a Roosevelt recommendation would be enough to get a student scholarship aid and/or admission.

Radcliffe, Vassar, Cornell, Harvard, Yale, and Berkeley joined Spelman, Shaw, and Virginia Union as colleges attended by Roosevelt graduates. Roosevelt graduates enrolled in more than 100 different colleges and universities during the past fifteen (1955-1970). They ranged from small all-black colleges to all-white colleges with only one black student, to large multiracial, predominately white universities. In 1972 in one midwestern medical school, five of the six black students enrolled in the first two years were from Roosevelt.

In every area, the results began to show. During the late fifties and early sixties, foreign languages broke the sound barrier. Thirty students are selected on a competitive basis by the State University Foreign Language professors for foreign language study abroad. Of the thirty selected one year, six came from Roosevelt. In the next five years no fewer than three each year were selected from Roosevelt. The school is now the magnet school for foreign languages for the city. The Roosevelt dance troupe, Orchesis, also went to Europe—on tour, with funds they raised themselves and from community contributions. They also toured many black colleges in the United States.

Only one coach in the history of the state has ever coached state championship teams in three major sports: basketball, cross-country, and track. He came from Roosevelt. This despite the fact that it was not until the early 1940s that black teams were permitted to compete with white teams in the state. Few high schools have ever produced more than two Olympic champions or world-record holders. One of those schools is Roosevelt. Until 1969 there had been only one black quarterback in professional desegregated football. He was a graduate of Roosevelt. There have been only three black presidents of the city council in Steeltown since its founding. Two were Roosevelt graduates. Of the practicing physicians and lawyers who attended schools in Steeltown and practice there today, a significant percentage graduated from Roosevelt. The first black city comptroller was a Roosevelt graduate. So are many of the businessmen, teachers, plumbers, and electricians. Four of the nine city councilmen are Roosevelt graduates.

Mr. T. had a dream, and, if he didn't do it all, he did enough. Under the most difficult circumstances, against almost impossible odds, he managed to give poor black children a sense of pride and accomplishment; a sense of their own power and worth. Maybe the times were different. Maybe he couldn't do it today; I wouldn't bet on it. The fact is he did it when it mattered, with the generations of children who were his responsibility. And that, in my view, is enough of a testimonial to any man's life.

Chapter Six

Advocacy and Education: Toward a Policy of Skills, Empowerment, and Humaneness

Senator Walter Mondale of Minnesota, speaking to the American Educational Research Association in February 1971, said he would like to know what worked in education. As a national policymaker, he was bombarded with arguments on all sides on educational questions; nobody seems to agree with anyone else's approach.[1]

Others, including parents, citizens, and teachers as well as policymakers and academicians, have noted the same phenomenon. When the education issue under discussion concerns the poor and minority groups, the situation is exacerbated almost beyond comprehension. It seems appropriate therefore to reiterate what to some will seem commonplace but, given the present state of controversy in education, to many would appear necessary.

First, public schools have always been middle-class or upper-middle-class institutions and have never served the poor and minority groups as well as the middle class. Cremin,[2] Greer,[3] Ayers,[4] Sexton,[5] and others too numerous to cite have, through the years, commented on this state of affairs. At the same time, however, the poor and minorities have always viewed and used education as a primary means of upward mobility. It is precisely for this reason that blacks, other minorities, and civil rights organizations made educational opportunity one of their major priorities.

Second, children learn more by going to school than by not attending school. While it is true that many things, and important things at that, can be and are learned outside the schools, the fact is that for most children many things are learned only by attending schools. Moreover, certain bodies of knowledge are learned best or more efficiently when taught in an organized way by persons competent to teach them. For the poor, schools may represent their only opportunity to acquire certain bodies of knowledge.

Third, educational literature abounds with descriptions of the pathology of the poor and/or "disadvantages." This literature has contributed

87

greatly to our understanding of why the poor and disadvantaged fail. Unfortunately and significantly, it has contributed little or nothing to our understanding of why schools fail or, even more importantly, how they may be changed to make learning more successful. Indeed, such discussion hardly ever comes up in scholarly literature. Somehow, it is assumed that failure is part of the child's responsibility, but success clearly redounds to the credit of the school. The literature devotes considerably less space and time to the issues of attitudes and values or to the internal life of the school. It rarely discusses the life enhancing value of education. It seldom discusses, in any significant way, what education could become. Most of the discussion concerns what is, the status quo. It seems that the academic conception of education is constrained much more by the measurement of cognitive skills: measurement of intelligence or achievement tests. Apparently, it rarely occurs to many academicians and scholars, nor to teachers and administrators, that education should be defined by what a student is after he has completed his lessons and earns his degrees and diplomas. Perhaps, just possibly, values, pride, self-confidence, the ability to reason and analyze and continue to learn are at least as important as those test scores and grades in which we place such confidence.

Perhaps, this myopia, this tunnel vision occurs because we fail to ask the right questions about education: What is education for? What kind of human beings do we want in our society? Indeed, what kind of society do we want to create? Then, and only then, are the questions we usually ask relevant and appropriate: what skills, cognitive and others, are necessary for all children? What level of performance is acceptable? What knowledge is of greatest value? How should it be organized? Who should teach?

Sadly, perhaps predictably, those who would reform education have too often been university scholars with little contact with public schools and the way they work. Many of the innovations originated with university scholars and academicians who wanted to develop programs and materials which were "teacher proof": that is, capable of working in such a way that teachers and administrators, the heart of the process of schooling, could not affect them either positively or negatively. The results of that fantasy are upon us. Read for example, John Goodlad's gloomy report on innovation.[6] The Ford Foundation discovered after pouring millions of dollars into public school reform that the human element was the critical variable which determined success or failure.

CRISIS, DESPAIR, AND SYMBOLIC CRUSADES

In the meantime, the public schools continued their downward spiral. In our urban areas, in schools serving the poor, in school serving Blacks, Chicanos, Puerto Ricans, and native Americans, the incidence of failure reached frightening proportions. Thousands of children graduated from high school unable to read or write or speak at an acceptable level for employment, manpower training or post-high school education. Alarmed and angry, parents of the poor and minority groups began to agitate and demand something better. Fueled by the tide of rising expectations, the so-called war on poverty, a more demanding job market, and a newly discovered sense of pride and activism, citizens began to demand more involvement in decision-making, more accountability for educators and, at the very least, basic education for their children.

For the more affluent, there were options: the suburbs, private schools, and parochial schools. For the poor and minorities there were demands for community control, parent involvement, and apiece of the action—in employment, textbook and material selection, pluralistic curriculum, and bilingual instruction. The response of school systems, institutions of higher education, policymakers and academicians was not long in coming. Alternative schools and programs, paraprofessionals, team teaching, computer assisted instruction, integration, desegregation, the house plan, new math, open classrooms, non-graded institution, and a host of other innovations which one might accurately refer to as symbolic crusades.[7]

When the dust had settled, not too much had changed. Yes, there were more minority teachers and administrators. Afro-American history and culture, bilingual programs, alternative schools and programs, and new textbooks and materials were visible, but the basic product of urban public schools serving the poor and minorities was not too different. Again we had failed to address the fundamental questions about schooling and education. There had been progress, but not enough.

When educators were unable to solve the problem in a few years, disillusionment set in. The days and years of high hopes and optimism gave way to a period of retrenchment, despair, and a retreat to privatism. And then slowly but surely into the forefront came the apostles of despair, of inaction of retreat. Suddenly, it became obvious that ours was a losing battle and therefore unnecessary battle. Education really doesn't make a difference. And "scientific" evidence was established to prove the case.

THE NEW ELITISTS

The critics massed to make their point. Jencks was the one with the greatest impact, but others supported his conclusions. Some even suggested that a reduction in educational expenditures would not be a bad idea.[8]

A new breed of educational analysts and academicians seem to be telling us that schooling is not very effective as a vehicle for social correction and improvement, as far as the poor and minority children are concerned. And yet, no one could convince these same scholars and most middle- and upper-class parents that schools do not make a difference for their own advantaged children. They demand and get, for the most part, the very best teachers, physical facilities, curriculum offerings, and other learning resources. This elitist attitude suggests that Jencks conclusions are fine for other people's children, not for mine.

A look at the critics themselves is instructive. Almost all of the critics, with few exceptions, are holders of the Ph.D. degree. Even such radical critics as Ivan Illich, Edgar Friedenberg, and the late Paul Goodman, all held Ph.D.'s and espoused the elimination of formal schooling for the disadvantaged. As Tanner points out, it is astonishing how so many educational elitists who, themselves, were of modest social origins, owe their present status in society to the opportunities afforded by the American educational system.[9]

Ironically, James Coleman, whose data Jencks and others have chosen to use to support their conclusions, reached a different conclusion. Coleman contends that children from educationally disadvantaged families and neighborhoods should have a superior educational environment to offset the effects of family and neighborhood. Such an environment, argues Coleman, would require a vast increase in expenditures for education, not only for the disadvantaged, but for all children.[10]

While elitist academic critics argue for abandonment of the educational system which has provided access to opportunity for more people than any other system known to man, other nations are beginning to imitate and adopt major elements of the American public educational system.[11] It seems that American schools, with all their faults, have accomplished more than any other of our social institutions. Myrdal observed forty years ago that the belief in education was part of the American creed and he went on to say that "education had always been the great hope for both the individual and society."[12] More than thirty years earlier, Dewey wrote: "I believe that education is the fundamental method of social progress and reform."[13]

And so the debate is joined between those who assert that our educational efforts should be restricted, based on the status quo, and those who argue for the life enhancing possibilities of schooling and education; between those who espouse elitist education for their own children and those who argue for the best possible education for all children, the poor and minorities included. To a confused and weary public these contradictory views contribute little to clarity. As forensic social science, they leave much to be desired in informing makers of public policy. A malaise, a sense of alienation, one might even argue that anomie is a more descriptive term, has settled upon the national conscience and psyche.

A NOTE ON THE PROBLEM OF OBJECTIVITY IN SOCIAL SCIENCE

It is of great importance, when examining the "new assault on equality," to keep clearly in mind the phenomenon described by historian Arthur O. Lovejoy

as "metaphysical pathos." Metaphysical pathos is defined as "the set of sentiments with which every theory is associated, but which those subscribing to
the theory can only dimly sense." Lovejoy was warning that "a commitment
to a theory may be made because the theory is congruent with the mood or
deep-lying sentiments of its adherents, rather than merely because it has been
cerebrally inspected and found valid."[14]

Modern social scientists have frequently stated that it is not only
possible but desirable to separate "facts" from "values" (particularly their
own). Only by eschewing intuition or subjective judgment, they argue, can
progress be made toward the establishment of social theories as reliable as
those which have permitted the physical sciences to advance so rapidly. But
in his quest for objectivity, the researcher (and his unwary or naive audience)
may too readily ignore the bias inherent in his selection of what to study, his
development of hypotheses, and his analysis of the data. Eleanore Burke Leacock
describes the problem this way:

> Social scientists aim to achieve an objective, detached, and truly
> scientific attitude toward society. . . .
>
> Unfortunately, however, the findings of their own sciences,
> constantly affirm the fact that, though they may constantly strive
> for the goal of objectivity, they should never assume that it can
> be completely attained. Social scientists are human beings, which
> means social and cultural beings whose needs, desires, fears and
> persuasions must impinge upon their work in various ways. By
> definition "middle-class", their scientific calling does not auto-
> matically make them immune to ethnocentrism when looking at
> members of the lower classes. Since the vast majority of social
> scientists are white, their attempts to achieve understanding across
> black-white lines are also subject to the chauvinism embedded in
> our culture.[15]

Similarly, John Kenneth Galbraith, in his 1972 presidential address
to the American Economic Association, called attention to the ways in which
economists become captives of their stereotypes—or of the prevailing political
tides. He said:

> Four years ago Mr. Nixon came to office with a firm commitment
> to neoclassical orthodoxy. In this he was supported by some of its
> most distinguished and devout exponents in all the land. His sub-
> sequent discovery that he was a Keynesian involved no precipitate
> or radical departure from this faith. The discovery came thirty-five
> years after The General Theory; as I have just noted, all neo-Key-
> nesian policy rests firmly on the paramount role of the market. But
> then a year and a half ago, facing re-election, he found that his
> economists' commitment to neo-classical and Keynesian orthodoxy,
> however admirable in the abstract, was a luxury that he could no

longer afford. He apostasized to wage and price control; so, with exemplary flexibility of mind, did his economists. . . . But our admiration for this pliability should not keep us from recalling that, when the President changed course, no American economists were anywhere working on the policy he was forced by circumstances to adopt. And it is even more disturbing that few are now working on the policy which we have been forced to follow. More economists, in fact, are still concerning themselves with the effort to reconcile controls with the neo-classical market. This has involved an unrewarding combination of economics and archeology with wishful thinking.[16]

Dr. Galbraith concluded:

I do not plead for partisanship in our econimics but for neutrality. But let us be clear as to what is neutral. (Current economic theory) is the influenual and invaluable ally of those whose exercise of power depends on an acquiescent public. If the state is the executive committee of the great corporation and planning system, it's partly because neo-classical economics is its instrument for neutralizing suspicion that this is so.[17]

Another characteristic of the so-called "value free" approach to the study of human affairs is its heavy reliance on statistics. It tends to "reduce" to numbers what some would say is "irreducible" (human motives, choices, attitudes) and/or to ignore data which cannot be quantified. Every beginning student of statistics is warned about bias in the selection of samples, the importance of accuracy in "operationalizing" hypotheses (that is, ensuring that the research instrument is capable of uncovering the information desired), and the difficulties of obtaining honest responses. Good statisticians not only heed these warnings but note any difficulties encountered as part of the final report—and, indeed, their findings are, by the very nature of the statistical method, reported in probabilistic terms. Unfortunately, even research which is carefully stamped "tentative" or "suggestive" loses its labels, so to speak, when it is picked up in the popular press or is adopted by advocates of a particular program. No thinking person would deny that the "scientific method" has valuable application to the examination of social problems, but we should not ignore either its limitations or its dangers—particularly the danger of accepting as "objective evidence" what may be the product of unstated or unconscious cultural bias. Such a caveat should not, and is not intended to, paralyze efforts to extend knowledge. Nor should it be taken as evidence of anti-intellectualism. Inquiry is always valuable and necessary if we are to avoid stagnation. But the understanding of the inescapable nature of bias should at least lend some humility to our own assertions, while giving rise to healthy skepticism about the pronouncement of others, no matter what their credentials or reputation.[18]

History, although not commonly regarded as a social science, is full of examples of wide variance in interpretations of events, interpretations which differ according to the nationality of the historian or which change in the light of new evidence. Think, for example, of the various ways in which school children might learn about the American Revolution, depending on whether they lived in the United States, France or Great Britain. Another example, of greater pertinence, can be found in the fascinating shifts in attitude toward the Reconstruction Period.

But acknowledgment of the existence of "metaphysical pathos" in the work of every social scientist is only half the battle: one must also recognize that any theory or set of data may be adopted by nonscientists in support of their particular positions. Even when social scientists abstain from any attempt to influence public policies, they cannot ignore the unanticipated consequences of their work, the uses to which their findings may, in fact, be put. A notable and agonizing debate still continues over the participation of atomic scientists in the Manhattan Project, or of biologists in work which may be utilized in germ warfare. Noam Chomsky, in his critique of Richard Herrnstein's *Atlantic* article, "I.Q.," underlines the importance of the "social function of his conclusions," and laments the "lack of concern over the ways in which these 'scientific investigations' were likely to be used."[19] If, Chomsky argues, a psychologist in Nazi Germany were to undertake studies which would support the Nazi belief in the inferiority of the Jews, his protestations of academic freedom and the right to pursue any form of research would be met with "justifiable contempt."[20]

When the theories of a particular social scientist are met with "extravagant praise" despite their possible bias, Chomsky continues:

> We are not dealing simply with a question of scientific curiosity. Since it is impossible to explain this acclaim on the basis of the substance or force of the argument, it is natural to ask whether the conclusions are so welcome to many commentators that they lose their critical faculties and fail to perceive that certain crucial and quite unsupported assumptions happen to be nothing other than a variant of the prevailing ideology.[21]

It is not enough, then, for social science to assert that since "behavioral science denies the very possibility of knowledge of what is good for man . . . questions of the goodness of laws are of no concern to these new scientists as scientists."[22] They must be willing to take responsibility for recognizing not only their own "metaphysical pathos" and their inability to be completely "objective," but also the unanticipated consequences of their research.

We have all become aware, whether we wanted to or not, of the myriad of problems, the litany of ills, the mosaic of pathologies. John Cogley, editor of *The Center Magazine,* has observed that our national mood has changed; we seem to have lost our confidence. The problems we now confront seem so complicated as to be almost insoluble. Even our visionaries seem to be going through a crisis of faith. The good life can't be ordered ready made from a catalogue. It seems we are going to have to do it the hard way, by trial and error, by making realistic choices among possible options.[23]

Andrew Hacker, noted political scientist, has commented:

> An awareness of problems need not lead to their solution. Indeed, too much comprehension can have the opposite effect. More and more of us are now part-time sociologists: we have no difficulty dilating on all manner of crises ranging from poverty and civil liberties to pollution and violent crimes. Whether in conferences, committee meetings or cocktail parties, we talk endlessly about fatherless families, generation gaps, sexual inadequacy, bad architecture, racial intolerance, subjugated women, bureaucratic bungling, the need for community and the demise of the American spirit. We are literate, knowledgeable, and as correct as any society has ever been in its assessment of its dislocations . . . (yet) sociological sophistication seldom prompts individuals to eschew personal pleasures so as to make society a better place.[24]

Understanding is essential. A lack of it confuses and confounds our best efforts to plan and implement new modes of operation. But understanding, too, is a means not an end. It may be that we have become so enchanted by the intricacies of describing what *is* that we have neglected the urgent need to explore what ought to be.

TOWARD A POLICY OF HUMANE EDUCATION

It seems to me that the *fundamental* question is not one of which program or approach is appropriate for the elimination or the mitigation of serious problems: functional illiteracy, dropouts, racism, opportunity. Rather, the fundamental question is whether we can survive as a nation of decent, humane, and free people. Recently, our theorists have been pointing out that the national malaise which cuts across generations of social or racial lines, is, at its core, a profoundly moral and spiritual one. The distrust and frustration, the anger and the hostility are not simply products of Vietnam or poverty, pollution or Watergate or discrimination. That we are faced with so many crises simultaneously may make our age an uniquely tragic one. But our real tragedy is our paralysis, a failure of faith in the ability to solve our problems.

Our expectations of unlimited progress have taken a very real—and probably richly deserved—beating. Maybe we need to become disillusioned with Madison Avenues' promotion of instant beauty, instant love, and instant success. Perhaps it is high time we stopped intoning that we have never lost a war. Maybe we need to call a moratorium on the quantity of innovative programs, of research and start thinking about their quality. Perhaps we need to start thinking about the quality of *people* rather than quality of our *leaders.* Carl Sandburg posed this question thirty-eight years ago when he asked:

> Who shall speak for the people?
> Who knows the works from A to Z so he can
> say, "I know what people want?" Who is this
> phenom? Where did he come from?
> When have the people been half as
> rotten as what the panderers to the
> people dangle before crowds?
> When has the fiber of the people been
> as shoddy as what is sold to the
> people by cheaters?
> What is it the panderers and cheaters
> of the people play with and trade on?
> The credulity of believers and hopers—
> and when is a heart less of a heart
> because of belief and hope?[25]

Belief and hope; how strange to hear such words today. These words do not fit conveniently in the computer nor are they easily assimilated into our grand designs for systems analysis, cost effectiveness, and massive organizational reform. These words have little meaning and no relevance to our debates over IQ, genetic inferiority/superiority, cultures of poverty, unheavenly cities, and wars on poverty. And yet, one is reminded of Congressman Ronald Dellums' assertion that it isn't guns and revolution which enable the poor and oppressed to get up every morning and face what they have to face, it is hope!

But, one will say, we are practical people. We recognize the accuracy, perhaps even the importance, of what you say, but what can be done with it? It is much too individual, too diffuse, too ambiguous. And my answer must be: yes, hope is individual, so is caring, so is belief. Belief, hope, and caring are neither ambiguous nor diffuse. They are real, precise, and their wellsprings are human and humane. Human and humane; two more words to confuse and confound. We all lay claim to being human, but what is it to be humane?

Herb Thelen, in a remarkable unpublished paper, provides some insight:

> The humane person acts with wit and wisdom, openness to ideas;
> he inquires, he appreciates, and he knows man by his achievements,
> accomplishments and aspirations. These characteristics distinguish
> man from animals and are therefore humane. . . . Mass murder also

distinguishes man from the animals, but this is *not* humane, for the second aspect is *compassion.*[26]

To be compassionate means to care and it means further to force one's behavior to be an embodiment of that caring; and what that means for educators—and this means all of us who care about education—is to pursue a policy of education which encompasses skills, empowerment and humaneness. Let us deal briefly with each of these.

Skills

There is a good deal of rhetoric today dealing with basic skills which to most people means the three R's: just teach them to read, write and do mathematics. Well, that is not what is meant in the context, although teaching students those skills is important. It means something very different and this meaning is much closer to the classic definition of skill. Webster's dictionary defines skill as distinction and knowledge; the ability to use ones knowledge effectively and readily in execution and performance. It is a *learned* power of doing a thing expertly; a *developed* attitude or ability. Even the archaic definition of skill is closer to this meaning than the cliches one hears today: it meant to make a difference, to matter.

Now clearly this definition opens up all kinds of possibilities. It means that education would provide the tools for learners of all ages to do expertly what they chose to do. This education would demonstrate that knowledge is *learned,* that aptitudes or abilities are *developed,* and that the ultimate value of acquiring such skill is to use it effectively and readily in executing or performing a given task, whatever it may be. One would therefore seek and acquire knowledge and skills as a *means* of accomplishing something he or she wanted or needed to do. By the same token, the educator/teacher would be required to see his role as a facilitator, a provider, a coach, a supporter, a tutor, as a person whose function is to help individuals acquire whatever is necessary to accomplish his or her goal, to achieve their aspirations. And, logically, the test of the effectiveness of this kind of education would be whether or not the individual can, in fact, acquire and use knowledge in the pursuit of these goals.

Empowerment

I recommend a policy which leads to *empowerment.* The dictionary defines empowerment as giving official authority or legal power. But, again, that is the least of this meaning. I prefer the other definition which means to enable; to make one able to do something. And this definition implies the *means* and the *opportunity* for doing. More importantly, this definition speaks not only to individual empowerment but to group empowerment. For the poor, the oppressed, the alienated, and the minorities, individual empowerment

is not enough. It is important, but it is not enough. No man is an island, someone once said, and that observation was never more accurate or appropriate
than when one looks at the degree of polarization, suspicion, and alienation
in our society today. It should be clear to us all by now that to be able to grow,
develop, prosper, and dream as an individual is shallow and unimportant if it is
at the expense of one's fellow man. For those at the bottom of the socioeco-
nomic ladder, individual empowerment is at best ephemeral and is at worst a
delusion. In a period of history when formerly powerless and so called "back-
ward peoples" can with a single decision alter the functioning of even the most
powerful nations—the current energy crisis or problem is a case in point—it
should be clear that the destiny of every American, indeed every human being,
is ultimately tied to the destiny of all of mankind. For minorities and the poor,
it is apparent that history affords ample evidence that our destinies are inextricably linked. For those groups specifically, and for the affluent and the
majority generally, it means that genuine empowerment must be a group
phenomenon, a group goal: in politics, in economics, in social policy.

Humaneness
Finally, I recommend a policy of *humaneness.* Education in this
context is marked by compassion, by sympathy and consideration for other
human beings; all human beings. Humanitarianism is part and parcel of this
educational policy. It is marked by a doctrine, an attitude or way of life
centered on *human* interests and values. The underlying philosophy of such
an educational policy asserts the dignity and worth of man and his capacity
for self-realization.

This policy of education openly and proudly asserts its concern
for the centrality of human values. It recognizes that people are never value-
less, never totally objective, always human. It asserts that wealth, status, power,
control, credentials, and intellect are secondary to compassion, sympathy, and
consideration for other human beings. It asserts that a person must be judged
first by his essential humanity, that each person, irrespective of his station,
status, age, sex, race or religion has an essential worth and dignity; his life is
precious and therefore to be respected and protected. It asserts that each human
being has not only the capacity, but the right to self-realization. And, more
important, those values would be consciously and explicitly taught, examined,
discussed, and respected. A policy of humaneness would become the organizing and underlying bedrock for all schooling and education. Without it, all
the other is like chaff in the wind. The arrogance of intellect is thus mitigated
and placed in perspective. As Sidney Harris, in a recent column discussing the
IQ controversy noted, "There has never been a society with too few intelligent
people; there has never been a society with enough *good* people."[27]

What we are talking about here is the training of men, and one
hastens to add that in this meaning the term is derived from mankind. It is in

no way representative of the male chauvinist tendency to ignore, exclude and denigrate the humanity, dignity and worth of women. Mankind includes both sexes. W.E.B. DuBois said it years ago. He was speaking about black Americans, but his words have relevance to all mankind:

> The Negro race like all races is going to be saved by its exceptional men . . . now the training of men is a difficult and intricate task. Its technique is a matter for educational experts, but its object is for the vision of seers. If we make money the objective of man-training, we shall develop money-makers, but not necessarily men; if we make technical skills the object of education, we may possess artisans, but not, in nature men.[28]

Skills, Empowerment, and Humaneness. These I believe, represent the bedrock of good educational policy and practice. But if this is true, it logically follows that the educational process must involve schools, the community, and parents, Each has its unique and special role and each has its unique and special responsibility. It is only through the open and honest interaction of all three that the young may be instructed in their human potential, even while they learn to moderate and question the arrogant pretensions of so much of modern ideology.

To accomplish this task, however, is extremely difficult. It is time to move beyond rhetorical and ideological battles. No single person or organization has a monopoly on truth, honesty or program. The choice is not between desegregation, integration, open classrooms or conventional programs, alternatives of free schools, words which have little meaning in and of themselves. Our real choice, it seems to me, is to define what quality education must include and act upon that or, as an alternative, to continue to react and flail against, individually and collectively, a system which more often than not ignores or denigrates human values.

But most important, through it all, we must remember that the struggle is about survival as human beings. Our ability to survive and continue to struggle has been sustained by our basic humanity. As our humanity has sustained us so we must now zealously nurture and continue to develop it. It is our youth we are concerned about most often, but in a broader sense the focus of our concern should be humanity. If our educational policies can enable our children and youth to become free human beings who can make choices, exercise options, and behave humanely, perhaps in the final analysis, we will have taken a giant step toward helping to free all men from the artificial constraints which threaten to make us all slaves, and therefore less than human.

We all have a part to play in creating Camelot. In the final analysis, it is each of us in our own lives who will demonstrate as well as speak our philosophy. The young learn by example as well as precept, from behavior as well as preachment. It is not innovations or materials or technology we need. Perhaps Professor Arrowsmith, formerly of the University of Texas, said it best:

> It is *men* we need not programs. It is possible for a student to go from kindergarten to graduate school without ever meeting a *man* — a man who might for the first time give him the only profound motivation for learning, the hope of becoming a better man . . .
>
> When students say that their education is irrelevant, they mean above all the absence of this man. Without him the whole enterprise is ashes, sheer phoniness. This is why students are so quick, and so right, to suspect a fatal hypocrisy in the teacher who lives without the slightest relation to what he knows, whose texts are wholly divorced from his life, from human life. What students want is not necessarily what they need; but in this case it is the students who are right . . .
>
> The irony of the situation is enough to make strong men weep. Here, unmistakably, we have students concerned to ask the crucial questions—identity, meaning, right or wrong, the good life—and they get in response not bread but a stone. Here we have a generation blessedly capable of moral outrage, and it is the bitterest of anomalies that the humanities should be dying among students capable of moral outrage in a morally outrageous world. Almost without exception the response of the universities to this profound hunger for education, for compelling examples of human courage and compassionate intelligence, has been mean, parochial, uncomprehending, or cold. Above all *cold*. The waste in sheer human incentive, in disappointment in matters where disappointment is destructive and fatal, is appalling . . . What, I find myself wondering, would education be like if humanists and teachers had the courage of their traditions and dared to face their students as men in whom their studies and texts found worthy, or at least attempted embodiment?[29]

Chapter Seven

Postscript

In 1966 the Congress of the United States was considering legislation which provided funds for rat eradication programs in urban slums. This was a difficult and crisis-ridden period in our cities, with riots and civil disturbances of all kinds either occurring or rumored. During the course of debate, a number of jokes and wisecracks reverberated in the halls of Congress. The amount of money to be provided by the bill was paltry: several millions of dollars at most. But the cavalier attitude taken by some of the congressmen angered many Americans, not the least among them, those trapped in rat-infested urban slums. Columnist Robert Raines, writing in *Renewal*, commented:

> Eradicating rats, of course, would not eliminate riots, It would only suggest that someone *cared*. The people in the ghetto have heard it loud and clear from our Congress, "We don't care about you and your children."[1]

Caring is what it is all about. What we have included in the three cases discussed heretofore; a few individual leaders, several hundred teachers, several thousand students. Not very many when one looks at the millions of students, teachers, administrators, and parents involved in public education in the United States; miniscule when one considers the billions of dollars expended every year. And what about the really important issues and their impact on the whole of public education: adequate financing, accountability, decentralization, community control, bilingual, bicultural education, balanced staffing, negotiations, the growing power of teacher and administrator organizations, reform and restructuring the system? These issues and their obvious implications for public policy should be our real concern.

What happens in the interim, before we solve the problems and re-solve the issues? What about the generations of young people who will pass through the system before we reach Camelot? What can parents, teachers, administrators, and students hope for in the grimy, boring, arduous, day-to-day struggle in ordinary classrooms and schools? Perhaps a lot.

Each of the individuals discussed in this book had to face similar questions during his career. The questions may not have been framed in the same words or they may have been stated in a different context; they were not too different fundamentally. In each instance the individuals faced them with a clear sense of direction, a battery of important skills and understandings, and they had the courage of their convictions. They faced reality; they understood that a few individuals have the opportunity to alter or shape the policy and practices of public education in any fundamental way. They decided, reluctantly, perhaps sadly, to do as much as they would within the constraints—and often in spite of the constraints—of their responsibilities. They understood, each of them, that each student was important and that his education could not be separated from his total welfare.

Perhaps even more important, these individuals understood, felt and acted upon something which may be crucial to all positive human endeavor: the quality of caring. They understood and believed that the most important part of the environment was psychological. They knew that teaching techniques, instructional materials and equipment, administrative style, and physical facilities paled in significance when compared to a trusting, caring, humane relationship between human beings: teachers, students, parents. The importance of this knowledge, this feeling, this belief cannot be overestimated, particularly when individuals act accordingly. Under the most difficult conditions, remarkable accomplishments are possible.

To argue that we need competent, humane people is to repeat a commonplace, a cliche. It is nonetheless worth repeating, because there are such people. The three people discussed in this book shared certain qualities. They acted out, in their lives, their commitment; not just in the classroom, but in all of their activities. They believed in the ultimate possibilities of the youth who were their charges. They took risks, they dared and, above all, they were advocates. They were men and women first; their roles as educators were secondary.

Jim, Laura, Mr. T., and others have met Professor Arrowsmith's definition of Men. They cared. They had to settle for something less than the ultimate. They compromised on some things and held fast on others. They made a difference precisely because they believed that an individual could make a difference. To the best of their abilities, they saved the children.

Appendix

School Program and Location	Information	Citation
Windsor Hills Elementary School	Three years ago Windsor Hills Elementary had the highest reading scores in the Los Angeles School system. The school has been constantly above national norms in basic skills. It is centered in a very affluent, black area; most of the parents are highly educated professionals.	Mr. James Taylor, Deputy Superintendent of Schools, Los Angeles County Schools Los Angeles, California Ms.Pamala Haynes, "Right On," *The Philadelphia Tribune*, Tuesday, January 2, 1973.
P.S. 129—West Harlem P.S. 192—North Harlem P.S. 146—East Harlem	The pupil achievement academically in these schools approximates or surpasses national and citywide norms. Students have a full rich and happy experience. P.S. 129 89% Black 10% Puerto Rican 1% other P.S. 192 30% Black 60% Spanish surname (Puerto Rican, Dominican and Cuban) P.S. 146 45% Black 50% Puerto Rican These schools operate without grim, material environments. Disruptive incidents are at a minimum; comparable to best suburban schools. The children are poor: P.S. 129—78% eligible for free lunch P.S. 192—65% eligible for free lunch P.S. 146—60% eligible for free lunch Each of the principals is white, Jewish, and middleclass; representative of the New York City principals as a whole: Seymour Gang, Principal, P.S. 129 Matthew Schwartz, Principal, P.S. 192 Martha Froelich, Principal, P.S. 146 Each principal has spent his entire career in the New York City schools; student population is large for each school (about 1,000-1,4000). Teacher turnover is low, only one is an MES school (United Federation of Teachers Special School).	Charles E. Silberman, *Crisis in the Classroom* (New York: Random House Publishers, 1970), Chapter III, especially pp. 98-112.

Banneker Project
St. Louis, Missouri

Dr. Samuel Shepard, director of one of the five elementary school groups in St. Louis public school system, started three track system in 1957:

Track I — high scores on standardized IQ and achievement tests;
Track II — average students
Track III — below average students who were given vocational and technical courses.

Project was located in a poor, slum neighborhood with high crime rate. 9590 of the 16,000 were black.

Initial test scores for Banneker showed 7% Track I and 47% Track III. Otis Intelligence tests for 1958-59 showed Banneker children with IQ median of 90.5 with 12.1% below IQ of 79. Shepard's program of motivation, home visits, telling teachers to ignore IQ and scores—led to gains.
1. 8th grades went from 7.7 years in reading to 8.8 in 2.5 years.
2. From 7.6 in language to 9.1
3. From 7.9 in arithmetic to 8.7
Track I children increased from 7% to 22%
Track II children fell from 47.1 to 10.9%
Median IQ raised almost 10 points.
Attitude change in teachers and administrators was the key factor: an inexpensive and uncomplicated approach.

Kenneth B. Clark, *Dark Ghetto* (New York: Harper and Row Publishers, 1965), Ch. 6, pp. 143-144.

*(Author's note: Later evaluation reports of the Banneker Project suggest that achievement gains were not sustained in later years. These evaluations, like many others, miss the point; The increase in achievement scores enable students to move into higher tracks, providing more options and these students took advantage of those options and remained in those tracks. This is a prime example of looking at limited cognitive data without understanding the importance of other variables.

Pre-School Program
Baltimore, Maryland, 1963

Mrs. Catherine Brunner, director for sixty children, four years of age in most deprived area of city. Every child who entered in 1963 began kindergarten the next year. These children did as well as children from middle- and upper-class families. In the 1st grade, they were superior in language and understanding of problem solving than other

Clark, *op. cit.*, Ch. 6, pp. 144-145.

Betty Showell, University of Chicago, doctoral student in Early Childhood Education

Mrs. Alice Pinderhughes
Baltimore City Public Schools
Baltimore, Maryland

School Program and Location	Information	Citation
	children from the same neighborhood. In the 1st grade 2/3 of the original sixty were in the top 50% of their class and 10 in the top 25%. Similar program in Baltimore has shown even more remarkable gains. Directed by Ms. Betty Showell, currently a doctoral student at the University of Chicago. Program continues its outstanding record under Mrs. Alice Pinderhughes of Baltimore City Public Schools. Success was confirmed by the United States Office of Education, declaring the program one of the top ten programs in the United States in 1973	
John Adams High School Portland, Oregon	John Adams is a district high school serving working-class and lower-middle-class students. A comprehensive high school and professional school concerned with educating teachers and educational research. Students are scheduled for only 1/2 day; the other half is spent in tutoring of basic skills, independent project work, work experience and elective courses as relaxation. Offers credit no credit, and conventional grades. The school is divided into four houses or sub-schools. Students are randomly assigned and instruction is interdisciplinary and general. Opened in 1969, the school is problem oriented. It is too soon to evaluate adequately.	Charles E. Silberman, *Crisis in the Classroom* (New York: Random House Publishers, 1970), Ch. 8, pp. 96-97, 103. Jerry Fletcher and John Williamson, *Research and Evaluation at John Adams High School,* October, 1969, mimeographed; cited in Charles E. Silberman's *Crisis in the Classroom,* Ch. 8, p. 369.
Parkway Program Philadelphia, Pennsylvania	The Parkway Program uses the city as a campus. Courses are offered anywhere: meeting rooms, library, university, museums, teachers' homes, businesses. Has its own	Silberman, *op. cit.,* Ch. 8, pp. 349-56. "The Parkway Program," The School District of Philadelphia, May 1969.

	faculty and university interns, but also businessmen, scientists, etc. The students plan their own education within constraints of the state law. Students are volunteers and are chosen by lottery. The program has had several evaluations by its staff, OSTI and accrediting associations. It is still too early to assess the long-term product although graduates have been able to enter college and the job market. The program is part of the Alternative School Program under the Public Schools of Philadelphia.	Cliff Brenner, "The School on the Parkway," 4th Friday Supplement to the *Philadelphia Jewish Exponent*, March 26, 1971.
Project 100,000 U.S. Department of Defense	Takes draft rejectees and teaches them basic skills to make them eligible for service	Charles E. Silberman, *Crisis in the Classroom* (New York: Random House Publishers, 1970), Chapter III, p. 98. I.M. Greenberg, "Project 100,000 The training of former rejectees," *Phi Delta Kappan*, 50, 10 (June 1969): 570-74.
Christian Action Ministry (CAM) Academy, Chicago, Ill.	Consortium of 8 Protestant and Catholic Churches. Located in decaying black neighborhood. The churches handle black dropouts, age 15-25, with less than 6th grade reading ability. 85% of the boys have police records; many girls have children out of wedlock. CAM offers three degrees: 10th grade equivalency, high school equivalency, and college preparatory diploma. Of the first 30 graduates of CAM, 20 received scholarships to colleges across the country. CAM has aroused considerable interest and has shown spectacular gains in learning and academic achievement.	Charles E. Silberman, *Crisis in the Classroom* (New York: Random House Publishers, 1970), Ch. III, p. 95-97.
Harlem Preparatory School New York, New York	The school is housed in a remodeled supermarket; offers only college preparatory	Charles E. Silberman, *Crisis in the Classroom* (New York: Random House Publishers, 1970),

School Program and Location	Information	Citation
	courses. Setting is informal, ungraded, and teachers develop the curriculum. The school demonstrates that informality, relevance and black pride are fully compatible with academic rigor. **Three tiers exist:** 1. 13 street academies in small storefronts, manned by two teachers and a street worker; go to job training from here. 2. Several academies of transition which prepare students for Harlem Preparatory or some other college preparatory program. 3. Harlem **Prep** where diploma is acceptance to college. Harlem Prep was originally sponsored by the National Urban League, which has a network of these schools across the country now under Experimental Schools Funding (NIE-National Institute for Education); and is being incorporated into public school system.	Chapter III, pp. 96-97, 103. U.S. Office of Education Dr. Robert Binswanger, Director Experimental Schools Program, Washington, D.C. National Urban League, Washington, D.C.
Northside Center for Child Development New York, New York	This center conducted crash programs of remedial reading in the summers of 1955 and continuing through to 1964. Data from 1955-1964 programs show that a child with one month of extra daily instruction can gain an average of almost a year in reading. Those with least retardation gained the most; those with 110 IQ or over gained more than two years, but most retarded children gained at least five months. The program was voluntary and attendance was never less then 85%. Upon returning to regular school, they retained gains but did not advance further. Served poor blacks and Puerto Ricans.	Kenneth B. Clark, *Dark Ghetto* (New York: Harper and Row Publishers, 1965), p. 140.

Junior High School 43 periphery of Harlem New York, New York	The school started Demonstration Pilot Guidance Program in 1956: Six times as many students went to college (25%). Dropout rate fell one-half from 50% to 25% 81% of the students were judged to have greater intellectual capacity than their earlier IQ and achievement scores would have predicted. IQ's in the 11th grade went up an average of 8-9 points. In the two year period during which tests were made, the average student gained 4.3 years in reading scores compared with 1.7 years during a similar earlier period. When one studies the project, one does not find revolutionary methodology. Most New York schools had both curriculum and individual counseling, field trips and programs for parents. The difference seemed to be due primarily to implementation of the belief that such children could learn.	Kenneth B. Clark, *Dark Ghetto* (New York: Harper and Row Publishers, 1965), pp. 141-43.
Dunbar High School	A black school under the dual system. During its 85-year period, 75% of its graduates went into college. During the period 1918-1923, Dunbar graduates earned 14 degrees at Harvard and Amherst. Twenty-four Dunbar graduates attended Amherst (7 Phi Beta Kappa) Twelve attended Williams (7 Phi Beta Kappa) Twenty-two attended Dartmouth Twelve attended Oberlin. Graduates included the first black general first black cabinet member, first black U.S. senator since Reconstruction, first black federal judge, and a significant percentage of the total number of black officers during World War II.	Mary Gibson Hundley, *The Dunbar Story, 1870-1955* (New York: Vantage Press, 1965), especially pp. 149-50. Thomas Sowell, *Black Education: Myths and Tragedies* (New York: David McKay Company, Inc., 1972), pp. 283-86.

School Program and Location	Information	Citation
	Parents of children attending the school were low level government employees: porters, messengers, clerks, postmen, and other jobs generally available to blacks during this period.	
Programs in Schools Throughout the United States	Dr. William Brazziel, Director of the Office of Education, Leadership Training Institute on Teacher Education and Early Childhood, Storrs, Connecticut, gathered information on quality education programs which exist throughout the United States. The documentation and description of these programs is contained in his recently published book.	William Brazziel, *Quality Education for All Americans* (Washington, D.C. Howard University Press, 1974). (Dr. Brazziel is Professor of Higher Education at the University of Connecticut)
Center for the Study of Student Rights and Responsibilities Dayton, Ohio	This OEO-funded legal services program was the only one directed by an educator, Dr. Arthur Thomas, and staffed by lawyers. It was also the only legal services program directed specifically at education and students. Under this program students and parents were apprised of their legal rights and responsibilities. Out of school youth, students in school and students having difficulties in school were taught to use the law to insure that they had full opportunities to acquire an education. The net result of this program was that educators as well as students were able to understand and use the law in pursuit of a common goal: quality education.	For further information contact Dr. Arthur Thomas, former director of the Center for the Study of Student Rights and Responsibilities, presently director of the Bolinga Black Cultural Resources Center, Wright State University, Dayton, Ohio, 45431

Notes

NOTES TO CHAPTER 1
DOES EDUCATION MAKE A DIFFERENCE

1. Daniel P. Moynihan, *Maximum Feasible Misunderstanding: Community Action in the War on Poverty* (New York: Free Press, 1969).
2. Edward C. Banfield, *The Unheavenly City* (Boston: Little, Brown and Co., 1968).
3. Nathan Glazer, "The Limits of Social Policy," *Commentary* 52, 3 (September 1971): 51-58.
4. Arthur R. Jensen, "How Much Can We Boost I.Q. and Scholastic Achievement?,"*Harvard Educational Review*, Winter 1969, pp. 1-123. See also *Harvard Educational Review*, Vol. 39, No. 1, pp. 449-83.
5. William Shockley, "Dysgenics, Geneticity, Raceology: A Challenge to the Intellectual Responsibility of Educators," *Phi Delta Kappan* 53, 5 (January 1972), 297-307.
6. Richard Herrenstein, "I.Q.," *Atlantic Monthly* 228, 3 (September 1971), 43-58, 63-64.
7. Hans Jurgen Eysenck, *Race, Intelligence and Education* (London: Temple Smith, Ltd. for New Society, 1971).
8. Herbert R. Kohl, *36 Children* (New York: New American Library Press, 1967).
9. Jonathan Kozol, *Death at an Early Age* (Boston: Houghton Mifflin, Co., 1967).
10. James M. McPherson, *The Struggle for Equality* (Princeton, New Jersey: Princeton University Press, 1964), p. 394.
11. Gunnar Myrdal, *An American Dilemma* (New York: Harper and Row, 1962), p. 902 (original publication date, 1944).

12. See Horace Mann Bond, *The Education of the Negro in the American Social Order* (New York: Prentice Hall Press, 1934). Also Robert L. Green, *Racial Crisis in American Education* (Chicago: Follet Press, 1969). See for an example, Ambrose Caliver, "Education of Negro Leaders," Bulletin #3, U.S. Office of Education, U.S. Government Printing Office, Washington, D.C., 1948. Also E. Franklin Frazier, *The Negro in the United States* (New York: The MacMillan Co., 1957). Also Henry Allen Bullock, *A History of Negro Education in the South* (Cambridge, Massachusetts: Harvard University Press, 1967).

13. The Carnegie Commission on Higher Education, *From Isolation to Mainstream: Problems of the Colleges Founded for Negroes* (New York: McGraw-Hill Co., 1971), pp. 31-32.

14. Select Committee on Equal Educational Opportunity, *The Costs to the Nation of Inadequate Education* (Washington, D.C.: Government Printing Office, 1972), p. ix.

15. See the Temple University Publication of the Census Bureau's statistics on the relationship between level of education completed and earning power. Cited in *Career Trends,* Temple University, Philadelphia, Pennsylvania, April 20, 1973, p. 5.

16. Edward S. Corwin, *The Twilight of the Supreme Court* (New Haven: Yale University Press, 1934), p. 20.

17. Robert L. Heilbroner, *The Quest for Wealth: A Study of Acquisitive Man* (New York: Simon & Schuster, 1956), pp. 171-99.

18. See, for example, the excerpts from documents relating to education (ranging from the Massachusetts education laws of the 1640s to the 1954 *Brown* decision and the early writings of Paul Goodman) in: *The Educating of Americans: A Documentary History,* edited by Daniel Calhoun (Boston: Houghton Mifflin, Co., 1969).

19. Daniel H. Chamberlain, "Reconstruction in South Carolina," in *Reconstruction in Retrospect,* edited by Richard N. Current (Baton Rouge, Louisiana State University Press, 1969), pp. 93-94.

20. See, for example, Leonard P. Ayres, *Laggards in our Schools* (New York: Survey Association, Inc., 1913).

21. Colin Greer, *The Great School Legend: A Revisionist History of American Education* (New York: Basic Books, 1972), p. 115.

22. Christopher Jencks, *Inequality: A Reassessment of the Effect of Family and Schooling in America* (New York: Basic Boosk, 1972), p. 255.

23. *New York Times,* December 1, 1972.

24. Jencks, op. cit., p. 8.

25. Ibid., p. 29.

26. Ibid., p. 87.

27. Ibid., p. 96.

28. Ibid., p. 159.

29. Ibid., p. 259.

30. Ibid., p. 256.

31. In addition to the critiques of *Inequality* noted here, see also *Christopher Jencks in Perspective,* a compilation of nine essays by prominent

educators published by the American Association of School Administrators, Arlington, Va., 1973; and *Harvard Educational Review* 43,
1 (February 1973), which contains responses to Jencks by a group
of social scientists and educators. It is important to note that student
achievement is certainly not the only criterion by which the effects
of school reform should be assessed. As early as 1968, Samuel Bowles
pointed this out in his article "Towards Equality of Educational
Achievement?" *Harvard Educational Review* 38, 1 (Winter 1968):
89-99.

32. Alice M. Rivlin, "Forensic Social Science," *Harvard Educational Review* 43,
1 (February 1973), 61-75.
33. Bayard Rustin, "Equal Educational Opportunity and the Liberal Will,"
Washington Post, October 1972, p. B-1.
34. James S. Coleman, "Equality of Opportunity and Equality of Results,"
Harvard Educational Review 43, 1 (February 1973): 129-37.
35. Stephan Michelson, "The Further Responsibility of Intellectuals," *Harvard
Educational Review* 43, 1 (February 1973): 95-105. Also see Otis
Dudley Duncan, "Inheritance of Poverty or Inheritance of Race,"
in Daniel P. Moynihan's (ed.), *On Understanding Poverty* (New York:
Basic Books, 1969). Duncan points out the income differential between blacks and whites despite equal levels of education.
36. Charles A. Asbury, "Yesterday's Failure," *Washington Post,* October 15,
1972, p. B-4.
37. Robert A. Dentler and Mary Ellen Warshauer, *Big City Dropouts and Illiterates* (New York: Frederick A. Praeger, Publishers, 1968). See
also *The Costs to the Nation of Inadequate Education,* a February
1972 report prepared for the Mondale Committee on Equal Educational Opportunity by Henry M. Levin. Using data from the U.S.
Commerce Department and other sources, Levin and his associates
estimate that males aged 25-34 in 1969 who had failed to complete
high school would lose $237 billion in income over their lifetimes.
38. Asbury, op. cit., p. B-4.
39. Gerald Grant, "Essay Reviews," *Harvard Educational Review* 42, 1 (February 1972): 109-125.
40. James Guthrie et al., *Schools and Inequality* (Cambridge, Massachusetts:
M.I.T. Press, 1971).
41. For a discussion of the Upward Bound Program see *Harvard Educational
Review* 43, 1 (February 1973): 40-41.
42. Henry M. Levin, "Schooling and Inequality: The Social Science Objectivity
Gap," *Saturday Review* 55, 46 (November 11, 1972): 51.
43. Alice Rivlin, op. cit.
44. Stephan Michelson, op. cit.
45. Kenneth Clark, "Social Policy, Power, and Social Science Research," *Harvard Educational Review* 43, 1 (February 1973): 113-121.
46. Gerald Grant, op. cit. Also see Robert K. Merton's discussion of the self-
fulfilling prophecy in *Social Theory and Social Structure* (New York:
Free Press, 1957). Also the work of Rosenthal and Jacobsen's

Pygmalion in the Classroom (New York: Holt, Rinehart and Winston, Co., 1968). See also James Herndon's discussion of how some teachers view poor black kids in *The Way it Spozed to Be* (New York: Simon and Schuster Co., 1968); a brillant discussion of this whole area is included in Eleanor Burke Leacock's *Teaching and Learning in City Schools* (New York: Basic Books, 1969).

47. Philip Jackson, "After Apple-Picking," *Harvard Educational Review* 43, 1 (February 1973): 51-60.
48. Rivlin, op. cit., p. 67 and 69.
49. Theodore Caplow, *The Sociology of Work* (Minneapolis, Minnesota: The University of Minnesota Press, 1954), pp. 101 and 121.
50. Charles Bidwell, "The School as a Formal Organization," in *Handbook of Organizations,* edited by James G. March (Chicago, Illinois: Rand McNally, 1965) pp. 972-1022.
51. Bernard C. Watson, *Stupidity, Sloth and Public Policy: Social Darwinism Rides Again* (Washington: National Urban Coalition, May 15, 1973).
52. *Social Policy,* May/June 1972, pp. 2-32.
53. Eleanor Burke Leacock, "Introduction," *The Culture of Poverty: A Critique,* edited by Eleanor Burke Leacock (New York: Simon & Schuster, Co., 1971), p. 18. See also, Alvin W. Gouldner, "Metaphysical Pathos and the Theory of Bureaucracy," in Amitai Etzioni (ed.), *Complex Organizations: A Sociological Reader* (New York: Holt, Rinehart & Winston, 1961), p. 79.

NOTES TO CHAPTER 2
THE SCHOOL AS CONTEXT

1. Roald F. Campbell, Luvern L. Cunningham, and Roderick F. McPhee, *The Organization and Control of American Schools* (Columbus, Ohio: Charles E. Merrill Books, Inc., 1965).
2. See Richard Saxe (ed.), *Perspectives on the Changing Role of the Principal* (Springfield, Illinois: Charles E. Thomas, Inc., 1968). Also see for a discussion of this subject: R. F. Campbell et al., *Organization and Control of American Schools* (Columbus, Ohio: Charles E. Merrill Books, Inc., 1965). See also, *Behavioral Science and Educational Administration, Sixty-Third Year Book,* The National Society for the Study of Education, Part II, Daniel E. Griffiths, (ed.), (Chicago, Illinois: University of Chicago Press, 1964). For an interesting reality test of the life of an urban principal, see Luvern Cunningham's "Hey Man, You Our Principal?" *Phi Delta Kappan,* November 1969, pp. 123-28.
3. See Bertram H. Gross, "The Scientific Approach to Administration, Chapter II in *Behavioral Science and Educational Administration, Sixty-Third Year Book,* The National Society for the Study of Education, edited by Daniel E. Griffiths (Chicago: University of Chicago Press, 1964).
4. Luther H. Gulick, "Notes on the Theory of Organization," *Papers on the*

Science of Administration, (ed.) by Luther Gulick and L. Urwick (New York: Institute of Public Administration, 1937).

5. *Dynamic Administration: The Collected Papers of Mary Parker Follett,* edited by Henry C. Metcalf and L. Urwick (New York: Harper and Row, 1942).

6. See, for example, Talcott Parsons and Edward A. Shils, *Toward A General Theory of Action* (Cambridge, Mass.: Harvard University Press, 1951); James G. March and Herbert A. Simon, *Organizations* (New York: Wiley and Sons Publishers, 1958); Jacob W. Getzels, "Theory and Practice in Educational Administration," Chapter III in *Administrative Theory as a Guide to Action,* edited by Roald F. Campbell and James H. Lipham (Chicago: Midwest Administration Center, University of Chicago Press, 1960).

7. See, for example, Barbara Sizemore's Statement to the Mondale Committee, July 27, 1971, Part 13, "Quality and Control of Urban Schools," Hearings before the Select Committee on Equal Educational Opportunity (Washington, D.C.: Government Printing Office, 1971); Marilyn Gittell, Statement to the Mondale Committee, July 14, 1971, Part 12, "Quality and Control of Urban Schools," Hearings before the Select Committee on Equal Educational Opportunity (Washington, D.C.: Government Printing Office, 1971); Bernard C. Watson, *Crusades and the Educational Crisis,* published by the Massachusetts State Board of Education; and the Greenfield Commission Report on decentralization of the Philadelphia Schools, 1970.

8. Derrick A. Bell, Jr., "Integration—Is it a No-win Education Policy for Blacks?," an unpublished paper prepared for the National Policy Conference on Education for Blacks, 1972, p. 18 summarized in the *Proceedings* National Policy Conference on Education for Blacks, edited by Bernard C. Watson (Washington, D.C.: The Congressional Black Caucus, 1972).

9. John W. Smith, "Some Afterthoughts Concerning the National Policy Conference on Education for Blacks," an unpublished paper.

10. Peter Schrag, *Village School Downtown* (Boston: Beacon Publishing, 1967), p. 178.

11. For a discussion of differential expenditures for schools, see Patricia Sexton, *Education and Income* (New York: Viking Press, 1961).

12. Marilyn Gittell, op. cit.

13. Barbara Sizemore, op. cit.

14. See, the Philadelphia Board of Education Greenfield Commission Report on Decentralization, 1970.

15. See Daniel Tanner's article, "The Retreat from Education—For Other People's Children," *Intellect,* January 1974, pp. 222-25.

16. An interesting dissertation in progress at Temple University by Bernard Rafferty, "A Status Study of Principals' Organizations in Urban School Districts," deals with collective organization among principals and supervisors in twenty major cities of the United States.

17. See Heinz Eulau's summation of the controversy in Michael W. Kirst (ed.),

State, School, and Politics (Lexington, Mass.: D.C. Heath Co., 1972), pp. 1 ff. Also see Arthur Vidich and Joseph Bensman, *Small Town in Mass Society* (Garden City, New York: Anchor Books, Doubleday and Co., Inc., 1958); Also see Robert Agger, "The Politics of Local Education: A Comparative Study of Community Decision-Making," *A Forward Look: The Preparation of School Administrators 1970*, edited by D.C. Tope (Eugene, Oregon: University of Oregon Press, 1962); Also Roald F. Campbell, "The Folklore of Local School Control," *The School Review* 68 (Spring 1969): 15 ff; and D.W. Minar, "Community Basis of Conflict in School System Politics," *American Sociology Review* 31, 6 (December 1966): 822-35.

18. For an example, in Philadelphia, the Italians, blacks, and Jews have favored their own organizations, each of which is competing for and attempting to influence personnel selection and placement in the public schools. See Lenora Berson, "Reading, Writing, Ethnic Infighting," Philadelphia Bulletin, *Today Magazine,* April 28, 1974.

19. See F. Znaniecki, "Education Guidance," *Social Actions* (New York: Farrar and Rinehart, Inc., 1936), pp. 189-230, 393-95; Also see the work on this subject by sociologists: Max Weber, *The Theory of Social and Economic Organization* (New York: Oxford University Press, 1947); Emile Durkheim, *Moral Education: A Study in the Theory and Application of the Sociology of Education* (New York: Free Press of Glencoe, 1961); Karl Mannheim, *Essays on the Sociology of Culture* (New York: Oxford University Press, 1956).

20. Charles Bidwell, "The School as a Formal Organization," in *Handbook of Organizations,* edited by James G. March (Chicago: Rand McNally, 1965), pp. 927-1022.

21. See discussion of how Dr. Marcus Foster carried out his role as a high school principal, *Making Schools Work* (Philadelphia: Westminister Press, 1971).

22. For a discussion of the origin and development of the Parkway School Program, see Clifford Brenner's article, "The School on the Parkway," 4th Friday Supplement to the *Philadelphia Jewish Exponent,* March 26, 1971.

23. Foster, op. cit.

24. Willard W. Waller, *The Sociology of Teaching* (New York: John Wiley and Sons Publishing, 1932).

25. An interview with a Philadelphia Middle School principal.

26. Richard W. Saxe (ed.), *Perspectives on the Changing Role of the Principal* (Springfield, Illinois: Charles E. Thomas, Co., 1968).

NOTES TO CHAPTER 6
ADVOCACY AND EDUCATION: TOWARD A
POLICY OF SKILLS, EMPOWERMENT, AND
HUMANENESS

1. Address by Senator Walter Mondale, American Educational Research Association Convention, February 1971.

2. Lawrence A. Cremin, *The Transformation of the School* (New York: Knopf, 1961); and idem, *The Genious of American Education* (New York: Vintage Books, 1966).
3. Colin Greer, *The Great School Legend: A Revisionist History of American Education* (New York: Basic Books, 1972), and idem, "Immigrants, Negroes and the Public Schools," *The Urban Review* 3, 3 (January 1969): 9-12.
4. Leonard Ayers, *Laggards in Our Schools,* (New York Survey Association, Inc., 1913).
5. Patricia C. Sexton, *Education and Income* (New York: Viking Press, 1961).
6. John Goodlad, "The Schools Versus Education," *Saturday Review,* pp. 59-61 and 80-82, April 19, 1969. See also Charles E. Silberman's *Crisis in the Classroom,* chapters 6, 7, and 8 "How the Schools Should be Changed" (New York: Random House, 1970).
7. See Bernard C. Watson's discussion, "Crusades and the Educational Crisis," published by the Massachusetts State Board of Education, 1971.
8. Daniel Tanner, "The Retreat from Education—For Other People's Children," *Intellect,* January 1974, pp. 222-25.
9. Ibid. See also Ivan Illich, *Deschooling Society* (New York: Harper and Row, 1971) p. 29; Edgar Z. Friedenberg, *Coming of Age in America* (New York: Vintage Books, 1965), p. 26; and Paul Goodman, *New Reformation* (New York: Random House, 1970), p. 88.
10. James S. Coleman, "Equal Schools or Equal Students?" *The Public Interest,* No. 4, Summer 1966, pp. 70-75.
11. See C. Arnold Anderson, "A Skeptical Note on Education and Mobility," in *Education, Economy and Society,* edited by A.H. Halsey, Jean Floud, and C. Arnold Anderson (New York: The Free Press of Glencoe, 1961), pp. 164-79; and C. Arnold Anderson "Access to Higher Education and Economic Development," in *Education, Economy and Society,* loc. cit., pp. 252-65. See also Tanner's discussion of this topic in *Intellect,* loc. cit., p. 224.
12. Gunnar Myrdal, *An American Dilemma* (New York: Harper and Row, 1962), p. 709 (original publication date, 1944).
13. Quoted in Tanner, op. cit., p. 225.
14. Alvin W. Gouldner, "Metaphysical Pathos and the Theory of Bureaucracy," in Amitai Etzioni (ed.), *Complex Organizations: A Sociological Reader* (New York: Holt, Rinehart & Winston, 1961), p. 73.
15. Eleanor Burke Leacock, "Introduction," *The Culture of Poverty: A Critique,* edited by Eleanor Burke Leacock (New York: Simon and Schuster, 1971), p. 18. Copyright 1972 reprinted by permission.
16. John Kenneth Galbraith, "Power and the Useful Economist," *American Economic Review.* Copyright March, 1973 reprinted by permission.
17. Ibid., p. 19.
18. For further discussion of this point, see Allen Wheelis, *The Quest for Identity* (New York: Norton, 1958); George C. Homans, *The Nature of Social Science* (New York: Harcourt, Brace & World, 1967); and Thomas S. Kuhn, *The Structure of Scientific Revolutions* (Chicago: University of Chicago Press, 1962).

196

19. Noam Chomsky, "The Fallacy of Richard Herrnstein's I.Q.," *Social Policy,* May/June 1972, p. 23, copyright Social Policy 1972 reprinted by permission.
20. Ibid., p. 24.
21. Ibid., p. 25.
22. Walter Berns, "Law and Behavioral Science," *Law and Contemporary Problems,* Winter 1963, p. 200.
23. John Cogley, "The Gods Keep Failing," in *The Center Magazine* 7, 2 (March/April 1974), 2-3. A publication of The Center for Study of The Democratic Institutions, Santa Barbara, California.
24. Andrew Hacker, "We Will Meet as Enemies" *Newsweek,* July 6, 1970, p. 25, copyright Newsweek, Inc. 1970 reprinted by permission.
25. From *The People, Yes* by Carl Sandburg copyright 1936, by Harcourt Brace Jovanovich, Inc.; renewed, 1964 by Carl Sandburg. Reprinted by permission of the publishers.
26. Herbert Thelen, from "The Humane Person Defined," Chapter in *Humanizing The Secondary School* (Washington, D.C.: Association of Supervision and Curriculum Development), pp. 17-34.
27. Sidney S. Harris, syndicated column appearing in *Philadelphia Inquirer,* March 25, 1974.
28. *W.E.B. DuBois, A Reader,* edited by Meyer Weinberg (New York: Harper and Row, Publishers, Inc., 1970), p. 158.
29. William Arrowsmith, "The Future of Teaching," *The Public Interest,* No. 6 (Winter 1967), pp. 53-67. Copyright c. by National Affairs, Inc., 1967.

NOTES TO CHAPTER 7
POSTSCRIPT

1. Robert Raines, "Riots and Responsibility," *Renewal,* September 1967, p. 6.

Index

About the Author

Bernard C. Watson is Professor of Foundations and Chairman of the Department of Urban Education at Temple University, Philadelphia, Pa.

Until 1970 he served as Deputy Superintendent for Planning in the Philadelphia Public Schools. He has experience as a teacher, counselor, department chairman and principal in the public schools of Indiana.

In 1967 he was appointed by President Lyndon Baines Johnson to the National Advisory Council on Education Professions Development and subsequently served as vice chairman of that council. He is chairman of the Urban Education Task Force of the National Urban Coalition, serves on the Advisory Committee on Education to the National Urban League. In 1972 he served as Project Director for the National Policy Conference on Education for Blacks sponsored by the Congressional Black Caucus.

His publications include monographs, chapters in several books and numerous articles in professional journals. He has lectured at many universities, served as a consultant for city, state and federal departments, foundations, businesses and community organizations. Watson received his baccalaureate degree from Indiana University, Masters degree from the University of Illinois and his Ph.D. from the University of Chicago.